THE JOY OF MOANING

A GUIDE TO THE EXQUISITE ART OF MOANING

DICK STROUD

CONTENTS

SETTING THE SCENE

The Joy of Moaning turns on its head the notion that moaning is undesirable behaviour, something to be avoided and scorned. Moaning is incredibly rewarding. It's the antidote to gloom.

· ——— · ◇ · ——— ·

L et me guess what interested you in the title.

Your partner, friends, family, workmates, maybe all of them, think you moan too much and this worries or annoys you? After a good moan, you feel a lot better and can't understand why everybody doesn't appreciate its enriching properties. Like me, you want others to see it as a positive activity, not something to be embarrassed about. Not only will this book make you a better moaner, but you'll astound friends with your understanding of this exquisite art. I cannot guarantee you will persuade them all to savour its rejuvenating powers but some will see the light and join the moaning community.

Perhaps somebody close to you is forever moaning? You want to know why and if it's curable or a permanent part of their personality. Can (should) it be stopped or made less annoying? If the chatter on social media reflects reality, then you are not alone. 'Is anyone else married to a moaning miserable old git?' is a frequent question asked on Mumsnet.com. The answer is lots and lots of people. I provide numerous ways to help your predicament. You can reduce the duration of the moans and the infuriating habit of griping about the same few subjects. Who knows, you might see the light and moan in tandem.

Some of you are searching for an amusing and inexpensive gift for a parent, partner or close friend, something a bit zany to make them laugh and you hope a book with 'moaning' in the title will do the job. I would be astonished if the book doesn't make them laugh – but beware, it might also make them a Grade A moaner.

Maybe you were intrigued by the title, especially the word 'Joy'? Having mastered mindfulness, healthy eating, Pilates and origami of your underwear (thanks to Marie Kondo), you seek spiritual enlightenment another way? Mmmm not sure the book is oozing with spirituality but it's brimming with insights into how to thrive during these doom-laden times.

Whatever your reason, I hope you enjoy the book. You will undoubtedly learn lots about moaning and have a few laughs along the way.

CHAPTER ONE
WELCOME TO THE WORLD OF MOANING

Moaning, a word of seven characters that describes a universe of complexity. This first glimpse of the subject will leave you wanting more.

. ——— . ◇ . ——— .

Has there ever been a better time for moaners? The reliable subjects of politics, generational conflict, turbulent financial markets, house prices and the weather are always there and a constant source of complaint. Of course, there is always English sport. Our cricket, football and rugby teams provide short periods of pride and aeons of disappointment. We have only been waiting half a century for England footballers to win a major championship. Hip hip hooray for the Lionesses. If you are an American reading the last sentence look it up online.

Just when anger over Brexit and certain American politicians was waning (a little) along came the nasty little SARS-CoV-2 virus to create a heap of new subjects for experts, 'experts' and charlatans to endlessly debate. Overnight we all became amateur virologists expounding 'the truth' about masks, vaccinations, lockdowns, testing and the stream of Greek-lettered variants. Each topic intersects with politics and the behaviour of politicians, adding yet more to the mountain of moaning material. Did XYZ politicians make the right or wrong decision, did they do it at the right time and for the right reasons? Did they follow the rules they had made? Were the rules necessary in the first place? Can you even remember what the rules were? Undoubtedly, you will know the answers to all these questions.

Then there are the latest topical subjects of climate change, wokeness, identity politics and all forms of 'inequality' with their idiotic/incisive views to defend/attack. All of these provide a 24/7 source of global news stories and social media chatter, creating an infinite amount of moaning fuel.

So many things to like and hate and we have yet to mention the timeless bedrock topics of angst – work, relationships, neighbours and, of course, people who walk their dogs without poo bags.

It's impossible to compare the moaning potential of different eras but I sense the early 2020s will be recorded as a premier cru vintage. What is certain is that there has never been a time when we could reinforce our prejudices with such an unlimited supply of news, curated to our exact requirements.

There is nothing more satisfying than plunging into a pool of opinions that strengthen our biases. *The Guardian* and *New York Times* are dependable sources for 'the left', providing a daily dose of new moaning topics, as do *The Telegraph* and *WSJ* at the other end of the political spectrum. MSNBC is the main source of news for Democrats; Fox News for Republicans.

If you want enriched moaning material you can satisfy your needs with filtered news streams on YouTube, Facebook, TikTok, Instagram, Pinterest, Substacks and the zillions of podcasts.

The technological wonders of social media are to be thanked for the more invidious and extreme sources of biased chatter that create a warm and cosy bubble of opinions, never threatening our prejudices, with ample ammunition for the next moan.

Rejoice, you have more things than ever to moan about and a free and inexhaustible source of 'facts' to keep the subjects burning bright. Alas, this abundance of gloom comes at a heavy price. Marinating in despair might energise the experienced moaner but, for many, it's a problem, a big problem. Levels of global happiness have plummeted, creating a surge in mental health problems. I tackle this thorny subject in Chapter 7 (*Moaning in unhappy times*).

Before we delve into the nitty gritty, let's start by investigating the basic question of why we moan.

WE'RE HUMAN, WE MOAN

Here's a little test for you. Think of all the words that can be substituted for 'moaning'. Don't take too long; you will have another chance to exhibit your vocabulary skills.

Extending the list to ten isn't difficult. Getting to 20 is more of a challenge. That's a lot of words to describe an activity, especially one with such a dubious reputation.

Reputedly the Eskimos have 50 words for 'snow' because of its importance in their lives. That's a lovely story but alas something of a myth. For whatever reason, we English speakers have numerous words for expressing displeasure.

Now list words that are the antonym (opposite) to moaning.

I bet it's harder than you thought?

If the number of words in the English language reflects the popularity of the activity they describe, then moaning and its variants beat its antonym hands down.

The more I looked the more convinced I became that we, well certainly Brits, are instinctive moaners. Ultra-lefties and those making Atilla the Hun look a softie, all moan a lot – probably about similar things. This doesn't mean they're unhappy or morose. They might be trying to make sense of the chaotic world, using it as a kind of therapy to release tension.

Moaning is a wonderful, unthreatening type of 'small talk'. Complaining about the weather, public transport and the rubbish on the TV is how we kickstart conversations.

In the next chapter (*Putting moaning under the microscope*), we'll investigate its multitude of uses and benefits.

FALSE ASSUMPTIONS ABOUT MOANING

I haven't completed a comprehensive search but found references to moaning as far back as the mid-1600s when the butt for the complaints was – surprise, surprise – the House of Commons. At the same time, Shakespeare had Ursula 'carping' in *Much Ado about Nothing.*

Over time, the popularity of words has changed, with carping declining and whinging surging in popularity from 2000 onwards. Our understanding and reaction to moaning keep evolving.

It was West Ham's most renowned fan, Alf Garnett, in the TV series *Till Death Do Us Part,* who was responsible for the contemporary image of an obsessive moaner. Then came the game-changer of linking 'grumpy' and 'old' – starting with the US film *Grumpy Old Men* (1993) followed a decade later by UK TV programmes, stage shows and books with the same name. *Grumpy Old Women* wasn't far behind. These shows employed a simple (and inexpensive) format of TV personalities, looking miserable, staring at the camera and moaning.

Let's dispense with the notion that moaning is a transitory

blip in human evolution – it's hardwired into our DNA. If we are not doing it ourselves, we get enjoyment from watching others.

Grumpy characters might be amusing and make good entertainment, but they have perpetuated the prejudices and become lodged into the received wisdom about moaners. These notions have crystallised as facts, but they are wrong, wrong, wrong.

Notion 1. *Moaners are unhappy.* Search for an image or emoji portraying moaning and you are presented with miserable-looking faces. The mouths are pointing down, they are scowling and looking angry. Characters in the 'Grumpy Old' TV programmes and films were always grimacing and annoyed. Never a smile, giggle or laugh.

Sometimes this is true, but a good quality moan elevates you to a position where you gaze down on the silly and naïve, with their daft ideas. Perhaps feeling sympathy for their foolishness, but laughter is the most common emotion. Knowing you are right, and they're deluded, is mighty empowering. Gloating is not an admirable reaction, but it's good fun.

Notion 2. *Men moan whereas women listen and fester.* Picture this situation. The man is grumbling about the same subject that he grumbled about yesterday, the day before and for as long as the woman can remember. She long ago stopped listening and radiates boredom, wishing she was anywhere but there. This is the stereotypical relationship between the moaning man and weary female partner. A regular scene in *Till Death Do Us Part* was Alf moaning and Elsie, his wife, moping.

But hold on a minute. Where's the evidence supporting

this much-repeated mythology? We will look at the research, but the simple answer is men and women could compete on equal terms in the moaning Olympics. I have no idea how all this will work out in our sexually neutral, self-determined times. Others can wrestle with that question.

Notion 3. *Moaning is an affliction of ageing.* Ha ha ha, you must be joking. Are teenagers bundles of unbridled optimism, positive thinking and goodwill? Do life's woes and shattered dreams transform them into replicas of their parents or worse still their grandparents, perpetually festering, never having a good word to say about anybody or anything? It's another one of those assumptions lacking a thread of evidence.

Are the young relentlessly cheerful – methinks not? Instead of labelling their incessant whining for what it is – moaning – we use excuses like 'it's all part of growing up' or 'it's their hormones' or worst of all 'they are so sensitive'. Stuffed with the illusionary self-confidence of 'going to uni' they prattle (a childish form of inconsequential moaning) about every subject under the sun.

For some reason, ageism hasn't joined the other 'isms' in that protected state of being a critical word where one fears to tread. Linking moaning and old is wrong. At a minimum, it deserves a trigger warning, perhaps a Twitter 'pile-on' and for repeated offences the 'cancellation' of the author!

DIFFERENT TYPES OF MOANERS

Was the ancient Greek maxim 'know thyself' first used in the context of moaning? We will never know, but this phrase perfectly describes the first step moaners should take to better use their moaning time. At last count, there were 64 terms describing sexual behaviour and orientation. Today's young must wrestle with questions about being Demisexual, Gynesexual, Bicurious, Libidoist, Asexual plus all the other exotic-sounding variants. Crumbs, life was so much easier in the 1960s.

By comparison, moaners are a more homogeneous bunch, fitting into one of ten categories.

The 'Live and Let Live' is very different from the 'Mega Moaner' who grumbles indiscriminately, not requiring feedback or confirmation, the stereotype used for the grumpy old film and TV series. The former is far more sensitive and aware of others' opinions. Once they have found a topic of agreement their moaning is as intense as any other.

Most people exhibit the characteristics of one or more moaning types. Over time the 'One-Trick Pony', the person who habitually moans about a narrow range of subjects, can develop into a 'Mood Hoover'. These people don't so much moan as frame everything in a negative light that can rapidly infect the attitude of friends and colleagues. This book contains a lexicon of moaning types, descriptions of their characteristics and hints to improve their moaning quality.

Like all behaviours, taken to the extreme, moaning has undesirable consequences for both the individual and those around them. Each moaning type has its own danger signals and possible treatments. Early intervention is key – all the more reason to read Chapter 5 (*What type of moaner are you?*)

SECRETS OF A GOOD MOAN

An important part of the formula for a perfect moan is having a partner or group of friends who are of compatible moaning types. Ideally, these moaning buddies share your views and desire to moan. If their opinions are very different you risk the moan turning sour and becoming an argument. A quiet unchallenging acceptance is OK but only if they conceal signs of boredom.

A period of moaning should be empowering and enjoyable. If you end up feeling more in control of life and having spent at least 50% of the time laughing it has been a success.

When you or your moaning partner becomes angrier, feeling more helpless, then something has gone wrong. Another unwanted outcome is when either of you exceeds your moaning threshold. This is a sign of having different moaning intensity and duration levels. Later, I investigate the dynamics of these problems (plus plenty more) and provide solutions.

Most people moan in a disorganised way. For instance, it's unlikely you match moaning topics to moaning partners – you should. I bet you don't have measures of moaning intensity – you should. You probably don't have 'red alerts' or define 'sandbox' subjects to ensure the moan doesn't become an argument – you should. If you feel that a period of moaning is like a cold and unpleasant shower rather than a long warm bath, luxuriating in confirmation bias, then Chapter 6 (*Moan like a professional*) is for you.

LET'S GET ON WITH IT

Self-help books usually have a couple of thought-provoking ideas and a few simple instructions that will transform the reader's life.

The Joy of Moaning is no exception. It turns on its head the notion that moaning is undesirable behaviour, something to be avoided and scorned. It delves into the detail of why we moan and most importantly provides a guide for doing it better. When you understand its intricacies, you are in control and with control comes a sense of empowerment. And we all want to be empowered.

Hopefully, the book should be fun to read but its messages are serious. You will be the judge of how serious.

Let's start by plunging into the details of what moaning is all about and put moaning under the microscope.

CHAPTER TWO
PUTTING MOANING UNDER THE MICROSCOPE

Like snowflakes, no two moaners are alike. Each moan has multiple dimensions and can be used in different ways. Gazing through the microscope reveals moaning's wonderful complexity and dispels our simplistic assumptions.

. ———— . ◇ . ———— .

U sing the Oxford English Dictionary (OED) is a humbling experience. The expanse of its research is awesome, as is its attention to detail. There are nine definitions of the verb 'moan'. Five of these are obsolete or rarely used outside the cultural wonderland of Scottish and Irish poetry, somewhere we're not visiting. Three of them refer to sounds made by humans and the elements. Remember to turn off the parental controls if you want to explore Google's zillion pages about 'men and women moaning'. This leaves us with moaning of the grumbling variety, the subject of this book:

> *Intransitive. Colloquial (chiefly British, original-ly Services' slang). To grumble or complain, typically about something trivial. Frequently with about. Also transitive, with clause as object.*

My knowledge of English (very basic) doesn't extend to explaining the relevance of the 'transitive' and 'intransitive' labels. I think it has something to do with the ability of 'moan' to stand by itself or requiring another word to complete its meaning. No matter, the essence of the OED's definition means to grumble or complain, typically about something trivial.

The Cambridge English Dictionary has a slightly different take on the word:

> *To make a complaint in an unhappy voice, usually about something that does not seem important to other people.*

Collins English Dictionary has yet another meaning:

> *To moan means to complain or speak in a way which shows that you are very unhappy.*

Merriam-Webster's dictionary just says to lament or complain.

All these definitions include the word 'complain', which the OED defines as 'To give expression to feelings of ill-usage, dissatisfaction, or discontent; to murmur, grumble'. What 'ill-usage' means is anybody's guess but 'dissatisfaction' and 'discontent' are understandable.

'Grumble' crops up a couple of times and means 'to complain about someone or something in an annoyed way'.

OK, enough of picking over the official definitions of moan. According to the experts, it's an activity that is:

- 'Something trivial' that is not important to other people.
- Said in an 'unhappy voice' or 'annoyed way' that shows you are very unhappy.
- An expression of dissatisfaction or discontent.

Good grief, no wonder moaning is so badly understood when the 'experts' have got it so wrong. Only one of these definitions is faintly accurate. If academia's guardians of the English language have made this mistake, I wonder how many other words are poorly defined?

Let's test the robustness of their statements. One of my favourite moaning topics is critically appraising the competence of politicians and economists. This is a nice way of saying grumbling about their ineptitude, deceitfulness and unwarranted self-confidence. Whatever you think of our current crop of politicians, how on earth can you say this subject is 'trivial'? Mistake one.

If this is not important to 'other people' – whoever they are – whose fault is that? Mistake two.

Who decided my state of mind was 'very unhappy'? What happiness meter was used to reach that conclusion? Mistake three.

So readers, within the first few pages of the book we see how academics, with their flawed definitions, have misled us about moaning. I very much doubt that *The Joy of Moaning* will result in the OED amending its definition, but I will send them a copy all the same.

This is Stroud's definition of how the word is used in the real world: Moaning is a conversational process ***not a state of mind*** where one or more people discuss an idea, event or person ***that can be trivial or important*** in a critical manner.

My definition differs from the dictionary in three ways.

Firstly, it separates the process of moaning from the mental state of the moaners. It doesn't assume they are desperately depressed or living in a state of blissful happiness. Secondly, the subject of the moan can be important or trivial. There is no absolute measurement of these words; they are subjective. What's important to me may be monumentally boring and trivial to you.

Finally, it introduces a condition about the contents of the discussion, that it is 'in a critical manner', a term that is similar to the OED's definition of 'complain' – 'to give an expression of dissatisfaction or discontent'.

My apologies if this section has been a tad academic but it is important to have a comprehensive and correct definition of moaning. Expressing the definition as a table emphasises the inaccuracy of the dictionary definitions:

Element of the definition	Dictionary definition	Stroud definition
Importance of the subject being discussed	Trivial	**Any** level of importance
Emotional state of the person moaning	Unhappy or annoyed	**All** types of emotional states
Nature of the discussion	Dissatisfied	**Critical**

TYPES AND INTENSITY OF MOANING

You might say that having removed the inaccurate parts of the dictionary definition I have simplified moaning to being no more than 'people talking in a critical way' and, to a great extent, you would be right. If so, what makes moaning different from complaining? To answer that question, we need to dive deeper into the factors distinguishing one moaner from another and to do that we need to understand the observable dimensions of the moaning process.

Imagine you're a highly intelligent fly on a wall, observing two people talking – one moaning, the other listening. There are numerous factors you could measure but these are the most important.

Intensity: How much of the dialogue is a critical commentary? It would be difficult, but not impossible, to give an exact measurement. Is it most of the time, about half, very occasionally, not at all? The elapsed time of moaning is a crude measure because it varies, depending on the nature of the conversation. Friends meeting to celebrate a birthday are likely to moan far less than workmates discussing their company's lousy managers. There isn't some universal set of rules about how we communicate, but we sense when they are broken, when the nature of the dialogue is inappropriate for the situation.

Believing somebody is 'always moaning' probably results from them exceeding the norms. However, maybe the person making the claim has become overly sensitive to the moaning behaviour. Yet more complexity.

Later we will return to the dynamics between the moaner and their 'audience'. This term refers to the recipients of the moaning – their friends, workmates, partners or any person or group of people they converse with.

Pattern: This is the most complex of the moaning factors and would tax our intelligent fly observer. How often is a moan used to initiate a new phase of the conversation? Are the topics of the conversation connected by critical comments? Does the critical dialogue reach a conclusion or is it left open? Does the moaner keep returning to the same subject?

You must know people (maybe it's you) who, when asked an innocuous question like 'How are you doing?' answer with a moan. Maybe it is justified but maybe it has become a habit.

Never is there a 'terrific, couldn't be better' but always a dour response. Another common behaviour is linking moans with terms like 'it's just the same as XYZ'. This happens so often that it has its own name – 'whataboutism'. One moment the subject is a complaint about the escalating price of fuel then it morphs into a moan about the economic effects of Brexit, which cascades into criticism of the Conservative Party and concludes with an expletive that we are all *****ed.

We all exhibit these patterns in how we communicate but in extreme cases the behaviour becomes habitual. I must admit to teasing good friends by introducing topics that I know will result in a moaning cascade. I start by moaning about topic A and can be certain that we will go via subjects B and C and end with D. Another ploy is to be overly positive about a subject that your talking partner always moans about. We might not like it but our moaning behaviour makes us worryingly predictable.

In Chapter 5 (*What type of moaner are you?*) we will look at how these patterns crystallise into a finite number of moaning types. Maybe you are a 'Detached Grumbler' or a 'Just One More Thing' variety, maybe even a 'One-Trick Pony'. You will soon discover the answer.

Type: Are personal issues or generic subjects the main topics discussed? Another way of viewing this distinction is the ability of the moaner to influence the target of their displeasure.

For instance, somebody is aggravated by the behaviour of their neighbour's children, who are inconsiderate, rude and noisy. This is clearly a personal form of moaning. However, it might be the starting point of a moaning cascade that leads to complaints about the 'younger generation' and then to the destructiveness of computer games and social media.

Generic subjects are outside the person's control. Moaning for an eternity about the taxation system and illegal immigration will change nothing, zilch, nada. It's this type of moaning that is most annoying to others, who can't understand the point in picking over events, people and ideas that cannot be changed. Worse still, always reaching the same old hackneyed conclusions.

Rational: Are the topics discussed in an objective and rational way or is the conversation a series of subjective and emotional statements? Clearly, there is a lot of grey area to this factor since it's not always clear when a logical statement becomes an unsubstantiated claim.

Buried in our genes is the instinct that tells us when criticism tips over into a rant. Before you jump to the conclusion that your moaning is firmly rooted in logic and evidence, think how many times you have moaned about some aspect of the pandemic. Overnight, people who struggled with GCSE maths and biology became experts in the science of virology and epidemiology, feeling empowered to moan about subjects that were baffling the experts.

To reinforce the aura of understanding they regurgitated mysterious terms they didn't understand. We must 'flatten the curve', always being fearful of a high 'viral load' that might erupt in the 'third wave' and above all guard against the 'asymptomatic' little critters that walk in our midst.

We can all recognise the archetypical pub bore type character, spouting their favourite prejudiced moans, or the red-faced, overweight older gentleman wearing red trousers who incessantly gripes about the bygone glories of the past. They are not that different from the person who moans by paraphrasing the last few articles they read on a subject they are ill-equipped to understand. Subjective and emotional statements come in all shapes and sizes.

Mood: Does the conversation affect the mood of the moaner? Our overworked fly on the wall will find this factor the easiest to evaluate. Does the moaner become angrier and increasingly disgruntled the longer the conversation continues? Or does the mood remain unchanged or lightened with increasing laughter?

You might say that mood changes relate to the person being optimistic or pessimistic and to the reaction of their audience. To an extent this is true but it's more complex than that. For instance, moaning about an overly politically correct television programme is something you can do nothing about other than turn it off. However, one person finds things to laugh about, like the actors who are perfectly racially balanced and the stereotypical characters with their stereotypical views, whereas another sees the programme as proof of society's decadence and the creation of a world whose values they despise. No prize for guessing who concludes the moan in the happier frame of mind.

By now you realise that the process of moaning is complex, with many variations. When viewed in detail it is very different from the simple act of complaining.

We will return to these factors in Chapter 5 to see how they define the ten types of moaners. For now, I want to investigate the reasons we moan and the emotional rewards it provides.

WHY WE MOAN

Years of our lives are spent moaning. Just how many you will soon discover.

In this section, I want to discuss why we devote so much time to complaining. The first thing to understand is there isn't a single reason, but six. We all have different moaning profiles, depending on how much time we spend on each type.

Usually, there is a dominant reason. Mine, like many others, is 'ego boosting', making it a good place to start.

Ego boosting

'Moaning empowers you' would perhaps be a more 'touchy feely' way of expressing this benefit. It transports you to a fictional world where you can criticise the great and the good using the scantiest of evidence. Better still, you are never forced to justify your arguments.

Yes, yes the consultant at the hospital might have 15 years of medical education but they didn't understand anything about my condition. I spent 15 minutes online and got all the information I needed and some more. What's so difficult about controlling the rampant rise in property prices, just implement XYZ policies and the job's done. Politicians could reduce inflation overnight if they stopped 'printing money'. As for global warming – what's the problem?; we know the solutions, let's just do it.

If only 'they', all the people you most despise, had your insights and determination the world would be a better place.

The country's sporting teams would be world champions, your friends would avoid disastrous relationships and so on and so on – if only they had listened to your critical analysis (moaning).

Achieving this boost to your self-esteem relies on a couple of things. Firstly, you must be able to jettison reality and fabricate memories about yourself and the world. Psychologists have a term for it – to confabulate. Secondly, you must be in possession of a moaning partner with similar views or who is willing to let your statements go unchallenged. You need a safe space, free from the usual rules of debate. University students are lucky since it seems universities have become one big 'safe space'. Be prepared for a future generation of super-moaners.

Your make-believe world collapses if your conversation descends into an argument and you are forced to justify yourself. Ideally, your moaning partner adds supportive comments to bolster your claims and feed the fire of your criticism. Failing this, they remain silent, nod their head and smile in agreement, preferably without looking too uninterested.

If only the world saw things as clearly as you do, life would be so much better, but alas, it doesn't. Maybe the Metaverse (the digital playground) will provide a virtual space where you can meet like-minded fellow moaners and put the world to rights. Never matter, the real world is filled with opportunities to bolster your ego.

Feeling virtuous

Many people – mainly the young, but with a sizeable sprinkling of baby boomers – spend an inordinate amount of their life promoting their virtue. Some might call it posturing. Rather than demonstrating their goodness by acts of kindness and personal denial, they achieve this by forcibly and loudly admonishing those seen (by them) as supporting the old decaying social order. The more you moan about what's wrong with society – and are seen to moan – the more secure is your halo of righteousness.

These people would never see themselves as moaners, but as champions of the oppressed (victims), defenders of the planet and judge/jury/prosecutors of society's nasties. With the fervour of religious devotees, they harangue (an extreme form of moaning) anybody questioning their ideals. Flaunting their title of 'activist' they indulge in unrestrained moral exhibitionism.

You might ask 'when does the expression of a strongly held view become a moan?' Let's answer that question with an example about 'inequality'. Believing that incomes should become more equal is a laudable economic objective. It's the boilerplate list of solutions that changes this from a worthy ideal into a stream of moans. The rich don't pay enough tax and should pay more (their 'fair share') – economic inequality is systemic and hard-baked into our society – the sharp-elbowed middle classes (the 'privileged') will always get to the top... That you might agree with the statements doesn't mean they magically become a constructive or realistic idea – they are moans. Good-intentioned moans (maybe) but moans all the same.

The same goes with achieving racial and sexual equality – or is it equity? Gone are the days when the solutions would be positive policies and building a consensus for change. Now it's achieved by admonishing the reactionary forces blocking the way with a tirade of moans coated in lashings of abuse. The ranting (the most extreme type of moaning) campaign against J.K. Rowling is the best-known example but there are many others who have been 'cancelled' and admonished. A few careless words in your tweet or 'liking' the wrong person and you're toast.

We all moan but it can become irritating when it's done in a smug, 'holier than thou' way. Ironically, those expressing their moral outrage the loudest seem to be the most intolerant of opposing views. Their way is the right and the only way. The last straw is when they indulge in 'luxury moaning'. That's griping about things that enhance their virtue and make other poor souls pick up the tab – usually those they despise.

For example, a common moan is about cars being the work of the devil that are driving (excuse the pun) polar bears to extinction. No policy to banish the gas guzzlers from the roads is too draconian. Waving your placard to ban cars makes your halo of virtuousness sparkle a little brighter and it costs you nothing. Living in a city, being young, owning a top-of-the-market bike, with a zero-carbon foot-print (naturally) plus an extensive wardrobe of Lycra, you will thrive. Those rejecting your views (the populists) live in rural areas, ten miles from the nearest supermarket with buses that run three times a week and suffer from rheumatism.

This all explains why the part of society – the majority – who haven't signed up to the dominant orthodoxy, spend so much time bellowing at the righteous that their actions are 'virtue signalling', a term that has become firmly embedded in our vocabulary since 2015. I prefer the phrase 'virtue moaning', which means 'loudly moaning to promote your virtue and achieve status'. Both these terms are fading in favour of the accusation of being 'woke', but that's a whole different story.

So, there you have it – your virtue increases the more you moan *and others see you moaning*. But there is one whopping caveat that's forgotten at your peril. What you moan about must be prescribed by the new moral guardians. These are a mix of academics (especially US academics), 'personalities', journalists and 'thought leaders'. This group is often called the professional-managerial class (PMC) but also answers to words such as: liberals, democrats, 'the left', progressives and combinations of these terms.

Not only are the names confusing, but so is the list of virtuous moans. Topics that one month cause the PMC to fly into a fit of anger are forgotten the next. These are known as transitory moans. Above all, it is vital to keep abreast of the ever-increasing list of victim groups and their relative importance. You must understand the mind-boggling rules of inter-sectionality (Google will explain) and practise maintaining a permanent grimace of anger and outrage.

Not only is the PMC the most effective group of moaners but they also define the language and moans of their hated opponents – who they call 'culture warriors'. Have you ever said something along the lines of 'Why is the media obsessed with language about sexuality?', 'there's more to economics than tackling inequality', 'whenever we have a bad storm or high temperatures it's blamed on climate change', 'why do TV adverts look as if they were cast from the UN?' If so, welcome to the land of reactionary populists. You are a prime candidate to become embroiled in the culture wars!

Gone are the days when divisions in society were about

family background, wealth and education. Now the battles are over symbols of virtue and their supporting moans.

It's all too easy to moan about this type of moaning so, before I fall into that trap, I will move on to the next variant.

Signalling group membership

Most adults are too busy getting on with their lives to be aware of or care about the type of virtue moaning described in the previous section. That said, we all use moans to signal to fellow group members we are one of them. Throughout life you are part of a generational group. Starting in the teenage years and throughout the 20s and 30s much time is spent moaning about friends and relationships – they never contact me – they won't stop contacting me – they are too serious – they aren't serious enough and so on.

Then comes work! I think HR departments should incorporate 'company moans' in the welcome pack given to new employees. Rather than having to pick them up, this would avoid awkward mistakes like moaning about popular people and policies and failing to join the pack as they ravage some poor soul who is deemed toxic.

For those having children, parenthood provides endless gripes about never having time to oneself – always feeling tired – partners not supporting with childcare – difficulty getting children into the preferred school – hopeless teachers etc. Fast forward to middle and later life when health and healthcare issues race up the moaning popularity list. These are often bragging moans – 'you are taking ten tablets a day? That's nothing; I am taking 15' – 'four weeks to wait to see a doctor, that's fast; it took me six months for a 15-minute call with the nurse'. Then there are mind-boggling boring moans about the unfortunate side effects of drugs and how the various pleasures of life are fast disappearing as physiological ageing takes its toll.

In the final years of life, when the moaner is not dozing, they complain about 'doing nothing but attending funerals' and never seeing their close relatives. You are probably thinking these are overly pessimistic generalisations. Perhaps; then again, maybe you are a maverick who has bucked the generational traits. Maybe you are a member of the group whose identity results from despising their conventional contemporaries and moaning about being grouped by age?

There are moans associated with our interests, like being a member of a gym. Favourites are raised eyebrows and complaints about inconsiderate fellow members, the cleanliness of the changing rooms and the place always being crowded when you want to use a cross-trainer at the same time as everybody else.

Choose an interest or pastime and you discover its own unique set of gripes. Boat owners moan about the cost of mooring fees, inconsiderate fellow boat owners and lack of good sailing weather. Those with sailing boats have an additional deep reservoir of moans about the type of people who own motorboats and, worst of all, jet skis. Supporters of sports teams opine about the quality of the manager, the inconsistency of the players and the cost of tickets. As for authors – their number one, two and three moans are about their publishers, who don't pay enough royalty and provide too little support.

Finally, there are activity-based moans. The most common and best understood are the stream of moans that erupt when people get behind the wheel of a car. You know these as well as me – the driver ahead keeps slowing down and speeding up – local councils leaving potholes in the road – random speed bumps – flashing signs that keep telling you to slow down – the list is endless. Different moans but equally predictable occur when we cycle or walk the dog.

It seems the signs of belonging are more often moans than positive shrieks of glee, which is odd, given that the whole reason for being part of a group is for the benefits it provides. We all want to belong and be accepted by fellow members by demonstrating our knowledge of the group's jargon and under-standing its humour and knowing when to laugh. Most impor-tant is remembering the group moans and their hierarchy.

A word of warning. Be very careful using moans to gain acceptance when you are manifestly not part of the group. There is nothing more embarrassing than watching a 60-year-old mouthing the moans of their children's generation in the hope of gaining acceptance. Like facelifts, it makes them look like an oldie wanting to be young.

I am sure you are thinking that your groups are nothing but sweetness and light and moan-free. Next time you are involved in a group conversation monitor the level of moan-ing. You will be surprised.

Exercising power

Steve Jobs, the founder of Apple, had a reputation for being awkward and complaining (or was it moaning) about people not doing what he wanted. His biographers probably don't use the word 'moaner', more likely portraying him as ultra-demanding and a perfectionist. Whatever words you use he was mighty successful, founding a trillion-dollar company and conceiving the Mac, iPhone and iPad.

He is an extreme example of exercising power by being demanding, critical and, as I am sure his staff would say, unreasonable. Steve Jobs is a one-off but TV characters have been built around these same traits. Bobby Axlerod ('Axe') in the series *Billions* deploys this technique to drive his hedge fund staff to outperform the markets. In *Succession*, Logan Roy, the brooding patriarch of his dysfunctional family, is in a perpetual state of grumpiness about the failings of his children.

Moaning to exercise power works for these real and fictional characters because they can bestow financial rewards, they are scary and rationing their praise makes it all the more valuable.

In the world most of us inhabit, this type of moaning is less dramatic and boring. Taken to extremes it becomes ineffectual and annoying. There are those people who will always find fault. You thought the latest Netflix period drama was brilliant; for them it was spoilt by the costumes, script, lighting, staging, choice of actors etc. They were so disappointed with the product – the one you had just been praising – that they sent it back. The inference always being that they applied more rigorous and demanding standards.

In a work context, there are colleagues, maybe your boss, who would always do a task differently and, by inference, better than you. You thought the requirements were XYZ; they were expecting UVW. This style of emphasising criticism and rationing praise is, in my view, the least admirable form of moaning. In our personal life, it results in the loss of friends. In the workplace, it verges on bullying.

The next time you are aware of somebody employing this variant remember the Dunning-Kruger effect. This sounds like some unwanted medical condition but is a much-observed human trait that people with the least capability are most likely to overestimate their ability and knowledge. It will not stop the person from moaning, but it will make you smile.

Lubricating conversation

The OED defines 'small talk' as 'polite conversation about unimportant or uncontroversial matters'. It's something we spend our life doing, a reflex action that fills those first moments when meeting new people. I bet you didn't realise that moaning is the main constituent of small talk?

Reddit, the social media discussion website, contains some amusing posts describing this form of moaning in action. I have paraphrased a selection of them:

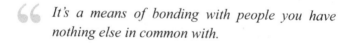

It's a means of bonding with people you have nothing else in common with.

Xmas cracker jokes are intentionally terrible because everyone moans at a bad joke, it's a bonding thing.

If you say something like 'can you believe it the train was late and there was rubbish everywhere on the seats' people tell their stories. Better than asking the boring question 'how was your week-end?' and getting the boring response 'not bad'.

Moaning about the weather is one way of bonding during a video call but much more fun to criticise the people who perpetually fail to turn on their mics.

These quotes suggest moaning is more than a social nicety but something that helps with 'bonding'. Since I never really understood what bonding was all about, I can't be sure, but it certainly provides a ready source of topics to lubricate conversation.

There are some rules for this type of moaning. It mustn't be contentious or require explanation and above all it must be self-evidently correct. The awful British weather makes it the premier domestic moan. It's too hot, too cold, too windy, too wet... Even if the weather has been perfect, you can moan about how rarely that occurs. And then there are the weather forecasters, who are bound to have got it wrong. I have an Australian mate who is convinced the term 'whinging pom' has its origins in the UK's meteorological conditions. We have had a long time to practise our weather moans; according to C.S. Lewis our obsession with the weather dates back to pre-1500.

You know the other small talk moans as well as me – public transport (regularity and price), the state of roads (gaping potholes and broken traffic lights), the latest political horror story and whatever celebrity has made an idiot of themselves. Failed politicians who rapidly morph into wannabe celebrities provide a heightened level of moan.

You are spoilt for choice with this last subject, especially around the time when those in the film industry prance about congratulating themselves.

Esteemed academics have researched this subject (University of Melbourne), in the context of the workplace, and concluded: 'Griping and joking themes invoke work experiences that all team members share or can relate to that make the team feel closer, at least temporarily.'

Using jokes rather than gripes is harder to do and contains more risk. It works in situations where you know about the people and their characters. However, some of us have the humour gene missing and venture into joking at our peril. We are all innately good moaners so, if in doubt, complain about the weather.

There is one more source of subjects to lubricate those first few awkward moments of a conversation. Global events that dominate the news are rare but they provide topics that complete strangers can talk about. Of course, there is Covid, the most-discussed subject in recent history. Then there are the global horrors of wars and natural disasters. As I was editing this section, Elizabeth, the queen of England, died. This was a global story full of moaning potential, mainly concerning the antics of Megs and Harry.

Very occasionally there will be something positive happening. Depending on your age this might be the finals of *Strictly Come Dancing*, the latest Netflix mega-series or the most-viewed video on TikTok.

A word of warning. Don't think too much about what you have just read otherwise you will start observing how different people navigate this process and start laughing the next time somebody moans about the weather.

Talking therapy

A friend calls or messages and says they 'want to have a chat' and will explain when they see you – sound familiar? How often have you been talking with a workmate and sense they are uncharacteristically anxious and want to tell you something but are holding back? Often these events are the precursor for a period of talking therapy where they talk and you listen, adopting the role of an amateur therapist. No doubt the roles have also been reversed and you have sometimes been the one with the unresolved issue.

We have lots of colloquial terms for this variant of moaning – 'letting off steam' – 'getting it off your chest' – 'a problem shared is a problem halved'. Not surprisingly, academics have wrapped fancy words about the practice and called it 'affect labelling'. The Catholic Church calls it going to confession.

When events in your personal or work life have resulted in stress and 'negative emotions' and you are – as psychologists say – 'pissed off', a prolonged moan works wonders. You can say all of those things you wished you had said (but didn't think of in time), bemoan all of the decisions you wished you had taken (but didn't) and harangue all of the people who caused the problem (but you were too frightened to blame them to their face).

The moan doesn't have to be about personal issues; it can be about life in general and how the country is 'going to the dogs'. Often the moaner longs for an idealised view of the past when they knew what was going on and felt in control. No amount of reassurance or logical argument is going to lift their gloom. They get comfort from their despair because it is predictable and a well-worn path they have plodded down many times before. Nothing ever gets resolved but that's how it has always been.

During these sessions, the moaning partner might add some useful insights and advice but the primary task is to listen and let the moaner vent their displeasure. Neither actor in this charade would say they spent a couple of hours and bottles of wine 'moaning' but rather that it was a useful time 'talking things through'.

The session ends with the moaner feeling better, at least for a few hours, and the listener bored senseless, but reconciling the emotion by thinking 'that's what friends are for'.

SO WHY THE NEGATIVE REPUTATION?

We have gazed through the microscope and observed the complexities of moaning and discovered how it permeates all parts of our life. So, why oh why does it have such a bad reputation and why is it perceived as something to be avoided?

The guardians of the English language must shoulder some of the blame for incorrectly lumping it with disapproving words like angry, depressed, cynicism, scepticism, pessimistic and worst of all 'being grumpy'. This inaccurate definition is not a recent development, yet moaning and moaners have only become things of derision during the past half-century.

There are three culprits for its recent demise – the fallacy that moaning makes you sick, the 'happiness culture' and Alf Garnett.

Moaning is bad for your health

Way back in 1996 scientists at Stanford University published research about the effects of stress on the human brain. These are quotes from their findings:

 Massive, massive amounts of stress or glucocorticoid exposure (medicines that fight inflammation) may shrink part of the brain (hippocampus) in humans.

There's absolutely no evidence that ordinary stressors cause much damage. And there's no evidence that stress causes Alzheimer's disease.

Did the observed effects result from extreme stress or did the extreme stress result from the shrinkage, something that could be caused by a neurological disorder? Their research was unable to answer this 'chicken or the egg' question.

Baboons, not humans, were the subjects for most of the research.

I have no qualification in neurology, but these findings seem straightforward and easy to understand. Journalists, however, are not known for their scientific literacy and often play fast and loose with the facts. Somehow, they managed to translate these findings into headlines reading: 'Moaning is bad for your health', 'Complaining is bad for your brain and body' and 'Moaning shrinks your brain, according to science'.

Not only does moaning 'shrink your brain' but it releases cortisol, which sends your blood pressure through the roof, locking you in a constant state of 'fight or flight'. Well, that's what the media says. This conclusion came from comments published by the Mayo Clinic, which believes **chronic** stress puts your health at risk (my emphasis). It qualifies this statement by saying that this all depends on your genetic make-up and previous experience of traumatic events.

The damage was done and the web became littered with articles and comments claiming moaning was detrimental to your health despite there not being a scintilla of evidence it was true. The mega myth was born linking moaning, depression and mental disorders.

Neurological science has been going through a tough time. In the past couple of years, it's discovered that depression isn't caused by low levels of serotonin, the chemical in drugs like Prozac. Whoops. Alzheimer's has long been thought to be caused by the deposition of sticky beta-amyloid plaques. I have no idea what that means but it now seems to be wrong, putting in jeopardy much of the research about this terrible disease.

What we thought we knew about the workings of the brain is forever being challenged (and rightly so). Journalists are always ready to interpret research to create an eye-grabbing headline. I think it is safe to say that moaning might or might not be programmed in your genes or might or might not affect your brain. Right now, don't ask scientists to be more precise than that.

Obsession with happiness

During my teens, as soon as Ken Dodd started crooning 'happiness, happiness, the greatest gift that I possess' it sent me scrambling to turn off the radio or TV. Don't get me wrong, I am all for happiness, the more the better; it was Mr Dodd's singing that I didn't like.

Since then, happiness has gone from being a natural, self-controlling emotion to something we 'should' experience all the time. If you are not feeling happy, then there is something wrong with you and the consequences are dire. What a ridiculous proposition, but one that provides authors and psychologists with a handsome living. By squeezing out of your life all critical thoughts and actions, like moaning, you are left with the residual essence of happiness; well that is the theory.

Have you ever wondered why your workmates always look so cheerful and full of glee on 20 March? They must be celebrating the UN's International Day of Happiness; or perhaps not. Maybe there are more important things the UN could be doing like alleviating starvation and stopping wars.

Come on, you stand more chance of finding the end of the rainbow than chasing the happiness gene, but you can waste a fortune buying a mountain of costly advice to help your quest. Failure and more unhappiness are the inevitable outcome of this fruitless pursuit.

Key into Amazon's search the word 'happiness' and you are presented with 100,000 products, of which 70,000 are books. If you are having negative thoughts then there are 9,000 titles that can help. A search for moaning returns 630 titles and most of them are about how to stop doing it!

It's odd, some might say disturbing, that the more we strive for something the less success we have in achieving the goal. Obesity levels are surging yet there have never been more books – 70,000 titles on Amazon – with the solution to shedding the unwanted kilos. Happiness might have become a national obsession, yet academics tell us it is at an all-time low. Chapter 7 (*Moaning in unhappy times*) discusses just how dire things are and why this is.

Moaning has become the collateral damage in the battle to put smiles on our faces and be perpetually happy. The medical industry even has a name for this fixation – 'toxic positivity'. This obsession with positive thinking and the silencing of negative emotions is not only failing; it damages the one emotion that could help – moaning.

Blame Alf Garnett

Now for a test for your knowledge of English literature. Ponder for a few minutes the fictional characters who epitomise the archetypal moaner. I have asked this question of lots of people and each time the response goes something like this, 'that's an interesting question; I am sure there must be lots' – a long pause – 'you mean all literature including Dickens and Shakespeare' – 'yep, all literature' – a longer pause – 'it's harder than I thought' – even longer pause. Finally, I get a couple of names who might have some traits of moaners but are a far cry from being archetypes.

Ebenezer Scrooge wasn't a bundle of fun, but stinginess and misanthropy were his main characteristics, not moaning. Puddleglum, the creation of C.S. Lewis, is remembered for his pessimism, but his character was more complex, with traits of cheerfulness and looking on the bright side, even when predicting the worst. Faced with a dangerous walk he mused: 'The bright side of it is that if we break our necks getting down the cliff, then we're safe from being drowned in the river.' He was definitely not a moaner.

Chaucer's character Dorigen was forlorn and grief-stricken, but then she had good reasons for her unhappiness. Read *The Franklin's Tale* if you want to know why. Mrs Bennett, in Jane Austen's *Pride and Prejudice*, is not so much a moaner as hysterical and self-obsessed. Shakespeare's Falstaff does moan but his main characteristics, other than lechery, are boasting and being manipulative.

The only character that comes close to the stereotype is Eeyore in the Winnie-the-Pooh books by A.A. Milne. He is critical and a cynic who seems to enjoy being gloomy.

It's much easier to name characters that brim with a naïve and annoying cheerfulness, or is it happiness – Pollyanna, by Eleanor H. Porte, Dicken's Mr Micawber, Paddington Bear, Jane Bennett (*Pride and Prejudice*) and Pangloss (*Candide*).

It is not until the 1960s that the fictional character Alf Garnett appeared on the UK's TV as the epitome of today's notion of an obsessive moaner. Before dissecting Alf's character and the reason for his creation let's spend a few moments answering the question, why did English literature have to wait so long for such a character to emerge? No doubt there is a PhD student, furiously working away, answering this question. Until their thesis is published (probably never) we will have to rely on my thoughts. That's the code for 'I have no proof that my rationale is correct.'

It wasn't until the last quarter of the 19th century that life expectancy in the UK rose above 40 years. At the beginning of the 1950s most people died within a few years of reaching retirement age. Between 1800 and 1900 the average Brit left school at 14 and worked well over 50 hours a week, at the same time raising families that were much larger than today. You need time and energy to moan, something that was in short supply for our forebears. Moaning was a luxury that few could afford. Staying alive and coping with life's challenges consumed most people's energies.

Think for a moment about how our access to communications has increased during the past 50 years, providing us with thousands of TV and radio channels and 24/7 access to unlimited data, images and video via our TVs, computers and phones. This is a very different world from my childhood, watching one TV channel, listening to two radio stations and having the occasional treat of talking on the telephone. Today's world is deluged with news and commentary that we can discuss at any time, anywhere. Theoretically, we are the best-educated generation ever with the time, freedom and technology to discuss whatever we want with whomever we choose. Every form of textual, video and audio interchange provides a moaning opportunity.

All of these factors combine to create unlimited opportunities to moan and so it's not surprising that authors and scriptwriters took to creating characters who thrived in this new environment. In my opinion, Johnny Speight, the TV scriptwriter who created Alf Garnett, was the most successful. Alf was the domineering head of his dysfunctional family in the TV series *Till Death Do Us Part* and its sequel *In Sickness and in Health*. Between 1966 and 1992 he appeared in 110 episodes on UK TV and rightly earned the accolade of being 'a household name'.

Dennis Main Wilson produced the series and wrote about his and Speight's intentions:

> *To hold a mirror up to the world. Let it see itself,*
> *warts and all. Garnett was to be put in the pillory*
> *of public shame. With his loud-mouthed bigotries*
> *he was to be the anti-hero.*

The TV critic T.C. Worsley didn't hold back his disdain for the character when he wrote about Alf in the *Financial Times:*

> *He is the rampaging, howling embodiment of all*
> *the most vulgar and odious prejudices that slop*
> *about in the bilges of the national mind. What-*
> *ever hidden hates, irrational fears and super-*
> *seded loyalties stand in the way of our slow*
> *stumble towards a more civilised society, Alf*
> *Garnett is the living, blaspheming expression of*
> *them. He is everything most hateful about our*
> *national character – xenophobic, illiberal, racist,*
> *anti-semitic, toadying, authoritarian. He's a flog-*
> *ger, a hanger, a censor, a know-all and a Mister-*
> *Always-Right. He is a positive anthology of*
> *unconsidered bigotry.*

What he didn't say was whether he enjoyed watching the show. I suspect not. A one-star rating at best.

Alf was created to give vent to the political and cultural views of Speight and the actor who played the part (Warren Mitchell). Both were self-declared socialists and unhappy (to put it mildly) with the state of the country. You could say Alf enabled Speight and Mitchell to have a monumental moan that lasted for nearly 30 years.

Alf was a royalist, nationalist, imperialist and, worst of all, a Conservative who believed the country was 'going to the dogs'. I feel certain he would have been an enthusiastic Brexiteer and probably voted for Mr Trump, although he wouldn't have approved of his haircut or odd orange colour. I dare not think what he would have said about Harry and Meg.

He detested the Labour Party and its trade union supporters. He was sexist and racist. A woman's place was in the home, including Mrs Thatcher, who he thought should be 'chained to the kitchen sink'. England was for the English. What he thought about immigrants and the Welsh would today be submerged in trigger warnings or edited out.

Giving Alf the opportunity to moan and rant about his caricature of opinions would have audiences in fits of laughter. There was just one small problem. Instead of laughing at Alf, the audiences laughed with him.

The BBC was horrified when its research revealed that a significant proportion of the show's audience thought his views were 'quite reasonable' and concluded 'that the series may have reinforced existing illiberal and anti-trade union attitudes'. Clearly this outcome was an embarrassment, and the report was trashed. A quarter of a century later the BBC was even more aghast when the Alf Garnett-like views it had attributed to Brexiteers won a majority and voted to leave the EU.

Moaning characters would never be the same after Alf and his long-suffering wife (Elsie), who was forced to listen to his diatribes. The success of *Till Death Do Us Part* was mirrored in the US by Archie Bunker in the TV series *All in the Family*. The show's creator, Norman Lear, held similar political views to Speight and hoped Archie's moans would be so extreme as to be ridiculed; like Speight, he was wrong.

Two other TV shows soon followed on Alf's success and featured a moaning character. *Steptoe and Son* was about a father and son who ran a rag-and-bone business. Today we would say they were self-employed refuse recycling operatives. The plots were about Albert Steptoe (the father) moaning and scheming to disrupt his son (Harold), who was always trying to improve his social standing.

Victor Meldrew was the moaning star of the series *One Foot in the Grave*. Forced into early retirement, Victor was constantly seeking new ways to fill his time but being continually thwarted, confirming his belief that the modern world had conspired against him.

In 1993 the moaning stereotype changed with the success of US film *Grumpy Old Men*. The term 'grumpy' was associated with the characters' moaning and it was the dominant part of the storyline. Following its success, a sequel (*Grumpier Old Men*) was released in 1995.

The role of moaning as a form of entertainment was further developed with the TV series *Grumpy Old Men* and *Grumpy Old Women*. Fictional characters were replaced by celebrities who spent the programme talking to the camera and moaning. Jeremy Clarkson and Rick Stein railed against petty bureaucratic restrictions, Andrew Marr and Neil Kinnock lambasted dog walkers' indifference to the toilet behaviour of their pets, Bob Geldof opined about the blandness of branded coffee shops, while Will Self was just grumpy about everything.

Most recently children's authors discovered the creative (and financial) benefits of putting 'grumpy' in the title of books. We now have grumpy cats, goats, tortoises, bumble-bees and dragons. And let's not forget the appearance of *Moaning Minnie*, way back in 1940, *Mr Grumpy* in 1978 and Moaning Myrtle – thanks to J.K. Rowling – in 1998.

I find it ironic that all these films and TV characters have contributed to our image of moaning as something to be avoided, yet all the programmes were comedies, the characters were endearing and they all made us laugh (a lot). No wonder we are confused about moaning and its role in our life.

So ends a rapid canter through the history of fictional moaning characters. When the patron saint of moaners is declared I bet he will have a moustache and support West Ham United.

- The dictionary definition of moaning is wrong. It makes false assumptions about the moaner's state of mind and what they are saying.
- Moans have five dimensions. They vary by intensity, pattern, type, rationality and mood. They are complex little suckers.
- Most people moan to boost their egos, some to feel virtuous; and everybody uses moaning to lubricate conversations. Some use moaning to exercise power and control. Part of joining a group means mastering their ritual moans. Discussing problems with friends is always accompanied by lots of moaning.
- Films and TV programmes have moulded our ideas about moaning and moaners. Nobody has done more than Alf Garnett in *Till Death Do Us Part.*

CHAPTER THREE
WE'RE HUMANS; WE MOAN A LOT

Fuelled by social media we spend a couple of years of our lives moaning, grumbling, griping, whinging, whining and all the other variants. No wonder the human mind has evolved to make best use of this time.

· ———— · ◇ · ———— ·

During a Zoom call on 8 February 2021 the chairman of KPMG told his consultants to 'stop moaning'. By the end of the week, he had resigned, saying he was 'truly sorry that my words have caused hurt amongst my colleagues'.

No doubt there was much more to this story than his criticism of moaning, but the BBC, *FT*, *Guardian* and *Times* all focused on these comments in their headlines.

In many ways, he was wrong to admonish his staff for something we all do, day in and day out. It is like criticising somebody for sneezing. In his defence, however, all he was doing was moaning about his staff's moaning. This goes to show that *the context and timing of moaning are all-important*. He got it wrong and resigned. For the unwary, even mentioning its name can be dangerous! Soon after, the head of environmental investing at HSBC bank had a mega moan about the inconsistencies riddling ESG investing – same outcome – now writing for the *FT*.

Moaning influences all aspects of our life and is an integral part of the human condition. We need to go beyond the analysis of Chapter 2 to discover the reason.

THE CHICKEN OR THE EGG?

Benjamin Lee Whorf – nothing to do with *Star Trek* – was a fire prevention engineer and in his spare time studied linguistics. He is best known for his theory linking language and culture. Thanks to him we have valuable insights into the role of moaning in our day-to-day life.

Whorf's hypothesis about language's power to mould culture states:

> *The grammar of each language is not merely a reproducing instrument for voicing ideas but rather is itself the shaper of ideas, the program and guide for the individual's mental activity for his analysis of impressions, for his synthesis of his mental stock in trade.*

The liberal use of 'his' shows that Whorf (1897–1941) lived before our obsession with gender-neutral language. However, what he postulated is clear – the structure of language and our behaviour are linked.

Let's conduct an experiment to test his hypothesis. Take five minutes and write all the words that can be substituted for 'moaning'. To get you started here are five of the most popular – complaining, grumbling, carping, whining and whinging.

If you're a Scrabble or Wordle fan you can easily double that number. My list contains 20 words and I am sure it could be extended. That's a lot of words to describe an activity, especially one with such a dubious reputation.

Moaning	Bellyaching	Beefing	Wrinching
Complaining	Bitching	Whinging	Rag-on
Grumbling	Whining	Ranting	Grizzling
Griping	Carping	Bleating	Maundering
Grousing	Mithering	Kvetching	Muttering

Grab a coffee and biscuit, or maybe a glass of wine and some crisps, and get ready for the second part of the experiment. Warning – this is going to be harder and might be distressing for those with pretensions to be crossword champions or English scholars.

Write down all antonyms of moaning (i.e. words having the opposite meaning). All you have to do is to take the sentence 'my friend never stops XYZ', where this friend is annoyingly cheerful and uncritical. You might know people like that – I don't – but think of the words that could replace XYZ.

I bet it was harder than you thought. You probably came up with some of these words?

Accepting	Commending	Ratifying	Applauding
Forgiving	Approving	Rejoicing	Recommending
Agreeing	Complimenting	Acclaiming	Endorsing
Praising	Assenting	Enjoying	Appreciating

Although they are grammatically correct, would you ever say: 'My friend never stops complimenting – forgiving – commending – rejoicing'? You might, but I somehow doubt it.

There are no prizes but if I have omitted any words, let me know by going to joyofmoaning.co.uk.

There are some phrases that fit the bill – for instance, 'thinking well of' and 'giving credit for' – but such ungainly grammar.

Another way of expressing the opposite of moaning is by using a negative term. Something like being 'uncritical', 'ungrudging', 'uncomplaining', but none of these options really works, all sounding clumsy, laboured English.

A philosopher might argue that when we communicate the default of our language is either neutral or positive. If this was true you would only need words to describe negative emotions. For instance, if you are watching somebody walk along the street you might say they are limping or stumbling. There aren't words that define their opposite since we assume people walk naturally. This argument falls to pieces as soon as you start reading the news. The human condition is anything but neutral or positive.

I appreciate the last few paragraphs have been hard going but trying to explain the workings of the English language is difficult. Stay with me, we are nearly there.

It seems to me that Whorf is correct and that this experiment demonstrates that the English language is structured to reflect our desire to moan. Of course, the reverse may be true, and moaning has structured the English language. I dived into the depths of linguistic theory to answer that question and retreated more bemused than when I started.

I'm not sure it really matters what came first, the desire to moan or the abundance of words that describe the practice. Instead, let's be thankful that we have so many evocative words at our disposal to express the subtle differences in the wonderful experience of moaning.

- Maundering – an introspective, low-energy form of moaning.
- Carping – moaning about the same few subjects in an endless loop.
- Bleating – moaning in a pathetic and obsessive way that irritates the audience.
- Muttering – somebody moaning to themselves at a barely audible volume
- Grumbling – moaning to communicate disagreement and unhappiness to the audience.
- Whinging – repetitive moaning about perceived injustices, normally of a personal type.
- Ranting – an aggressive, out of control, variety of moaning.

- Bitching – moaning in a spiteful and malicious way.
- Griping – similar to 'carping' but more annoying to the audience.

I feel sure that some of these words are onomatopoeias (i.e. imitating the sound they describe). For certain they are expressive and meaty words. It can't be an accident that the English language has provided us with this treasure trove of wonderful words. Benjamin Lee Whorf was right – language and culture are integrally linked.

MOANING = COMPLAINING + ATTITUDE

As words travel through time their meaning is transformed by the dominant culture. For example, for centuries the word 'gay' meant being light-hearted and carefree. Then in the 1930s it started to change and by the 1960s meant one thing – being a homosexual.

'Woke' is an innocuous word you might have mixed up with 'wake' (no longer asleep). During the 1970s it was adopted by American counter-culture and given a special meaning. Actually, the change started much earlier (1900s) but don't let's confuse matters. Having jettisoned its association with sleep it started to mean being 'woken' up or sensitised to issues of justice, mainly those involving race. Now, drenched in political innuendo, the word means being ultra-politically correct and obsessed with parading self-virtue. In 2022, Kings College London found that 36% of Brits thought being called 'woke' was an insult, up from 24% two years earlier.

These are examples of words whose meaning has completely changed, but there is another affliction they can experience. Like money, they can suffer from inflation. Once upon a time, 'fury' described fierce passion, a disorder or tumult of mind. Now it means being very annoyed. A 'victim' was once somebody suffering extreme hardship caused by an oppressive or destructive agency. Now it describes numerous racial or sexual groups. A 'revelation' was once a disclosure or communication by divine or supernatural means. Now it means the latest thing a journalist discovered. Feeling 'exhausted' is to drain a person of strength or resources; now it means feeling a tad tired. Probably because of Covid, the word 'epidemic' has soared in popularity. Rather than meaning an acute disease affecting many individuals, it's used to describe a few instances of something occurring.

The language is also being mangled by those desperate to guard against 'giving offence'. UK local government is being instructed to substitute 'birthing parents' for 'mum and dad' and to banish 'homeless', 'lifestyle choice' and 'economic migrant' to word purgatory.

I could say that I am concerned about the way words are being banned and misused, but in keeping with today's fashion of exaggeration will use the word devastated, or should it be shocked, maybe even traumatised? There's a theory that this is some fiendish agenda to destabilise the language. Stripping words of a shared meaning makes it harder to have any form of reasoned discussion – remember 'Newspeak' in Orwell's *1984*? Having never subscribed to conspiracy theories, I think Hanlon's Razor provides the explanation – never attribute to malice that which is adequately explained by stupidity.

Once you become conscious of this word inflation you see it everywhere in how people write and speak. These words are especially popular and are bandied about like confetti with no thought to their proper meaning: survivor, vulnerable, toxic, poverty, blunder, crisis, disaster, chaos, bigot, racist, catastrophic, systemic, institutionalised and the much-used phrase, being diverse, inclusive and accessible. Whoops nearly forgot, the favourite ingredient of 'word salads' – sustainability.

Moaning and associated words have not been immune from the ravages of time, which is not surprising since some of them have been around for centuries. According to the OED this is when they were first used: complain (1373), grumble (1585), rant (1602) and moan (1628).

In the previous chapter, I defined moaning as: 'a conversational process where one or more people discuss an idea, event or person in a critical manner'. In other words, they are 'complaining'.

Thanks to the wonders of Google's Ngram search engine we can unravel how its meaning has become corrupted. (I won't bore you with a long description of how this technology works; you can look it up if you're interested.)

This chart shows the frequency of the word 'complaining' between 1600 and 2020, derived by analysing 8 million books, containing billions of words.

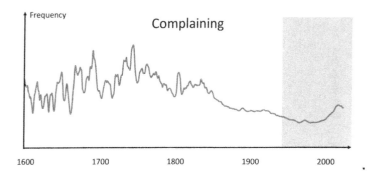

You don't need to be a statistical genius to see how its popularity has changed. Since the mid-1700s the frequency of use has been in decline, with a small uptick in recent times. Why on earth did this happen if complaining is so important?

The answer is graphically displayed in the following charts, also plotted using Ngram. These show the popularity of the words grumpy, moaning and whinging.

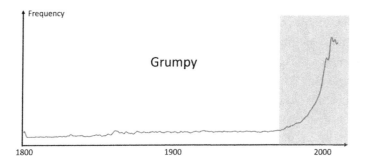

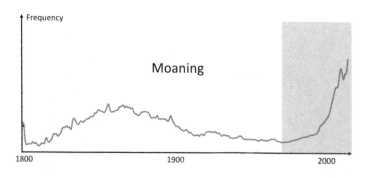

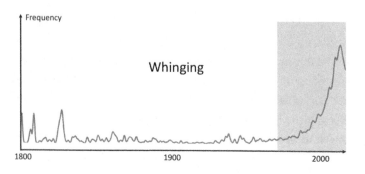

One simple conclusion shouts out from these charts. Over time 'complaining' has been replaced by more emotive words. As we have seen, the official definition of moaning is complaining about trivial matters in an unhappy way. Whinging is complaining in a 'shrill and querulous tone'. If these charts are to be believed, then authors felt impelled to replace the simple word with terms that made judgements about the importance of the matters being discussed and the state of mind of those involved.

You are probably thinking 'OK, and why is this important to me?'

Since we first rubbed a couple of sticks together to make fire, complaining has been a driver of human advancement. To be dissatisfied and to strive for better things has driven our progress. I doubt if our Stone Age ancestors discovered fire while they were decorating their cave or searching for self-fulfilment. No, being cold and the ravages of the elements would have been responsible, plus a liking for rarely cooked fillets of woolly mammoth, rather than raw fish and berries.

Complaining about the status quo and wanting change are vital to our continuing existence.

When complaining morphs into an activity that is tainted with judgements about the mental state of the complainer and the importance of their complaint, that blunts its effectiveness. That's why these charts are so important. Where would we be if the enterprising cave dweller, trying to perfect rubbing two sticks together, had been perpetually accused of being miserable about the cold and obsessed with trivialities?

When I started writing *The Joy of Moaning* I didn't realise I might be investigating such a fundamental aspect of humankind. Complaining is a vital emotion that drives us forward. We dilute its effectiveness at our peril.

MECHANISTIC MINDS

The hero of the science fiction film *The Matrix* is given the option of swallowing a red or blue pill. If he chooses red, he will see the actual and disturbing reality of his existence. The blue pill keeps him in a state of contented ignorance.

If you are wedded to the notion that we are rational beings, forming our opinions and beliefs after extensive research and consideration, evaluating the evidence and reaching informed decisions, then the blue pill is for you. Jump straight to the next section.

However, if when talking with friends and workmates you sense their objectivity is – what shall we say – simplistic and distorted… That you keep experiencing déjà vu, a weird sense of predictability about your conversations as if you are going through a familiar ritual… You keep thinking, 'Haven't they said all this before, lots of times and my response is always the same?'

If you want to know what's happening, then unwrap the red pill and swallow. Take a deep breath and read on.

What do you think about the conflict between Russia and Ukraine? Was the politicians' handling of the pandemic a mess or a superb achievement? Which is the better football side, Manchester United or Norwich City – sorry, that is too easy – Manchester City or Liverpool? Is Waitrose an over-priced store for the prosperous middle classes or an exemplar supplier for the environmentally concerned consumer? Are electric cars how the well-heeled placate their guilt about trashing the planet or a natural and necessary evolution of road transport?

I expect you have views on most of these subjects, perhaps with the exception of the football example. Substitute a question from the sport of your choice; is Federer, Nadal or Djokovic the greatest of all time, was Michael Schumacher a better F1 driver than Lewis Hamilton etc?

When you discuss and moan about these questions you are

not deploying any special knowledge or insights; rather your mind is performing a series of shortcuts to reach an answer. Even the brightest and most knowledgeable among us can't understand the myriad of issues that bombard our daily lives. Most of us don't even make a pretence of trying to reach an informed, let alone a balanced, decision.

For instance, you are talking with a friend about the latest gloomy economic forecasts and what politicians propose to do about them. For starters, you will automatically focus on the worst of the news. Neither of you is likely to have seen the relevant documents and have a comprehensive under-standing of all the facts. Your views will be determined by whatever biased source of news keeps you informed and your existing prejudices about the competence of the politi-cians involved. You will have (probably unconsciously) ignored, forgotten or diminished in importance any informa-tion that conflicts with your existing views. Finally, you are only likely to discuss the issue with somebody who shares your views, so you are unlikely to hear any opposing arguments.

How on earth do you change your views when they have been formed in this mechanistic way? Jonathan Swift's words eloquently expressed the problem: 'Reasoning will never make a man correct an ill opinion, which by reasoning he never acquired.'

I hope this description of the interaction doesn't offend you, making you sound more like a high-functioning machine than the ultra-bright, well-informed person you think you are. I bet you are having second thoughts about your choice of pill.

We all get through our busy lives by employing mental

shortcuts and moaning is an important part of this cognitive armoury. Here is a (very) brief summary of how it all works.

Addicted to bad news

Daniel Kahneman, an Israeli psychologist and Nobel Prize winner, explains it this way: 'The brains of humans contain a mechanism that is designed to give priority to bad news.'

Tracy Jamal Morgan, the American stand-up comedian, expresses it slightly differently: 'Bad news travels at the speed of light; good news travels like molasses.'

Both are talking about the 'negativity bias'. When sieving through new information we don't 'take the good with the bad' but spend more time and energy on the worst bits. It's as simple as that.

This human trait helps explain why moaning feels like such a natural condition. Just think how different our behaviour would be, how much harder it would be for moaners, if the bias was positive, not negative.

Those controlling the news channels and social media instinctively understand this human trait and use it to good effect. They are incentivised to maximise time and engagement on their platforms and being negative is their default. A journalist at the *Washington Post* captured perfectly the sentiment when explaining why their paper contains so many negative headlines: 'negativity is clicky'.

Back in the days, 'the story was the boss' – now news channels sell a narrative that resonates with their target demographic. Journalism has morphed into political entertainment that is inherently negative.

There were few positives resulting from the pandemic, but one was the unlimited supply of Covid stories the news channels fought over to display in their scariest form. Their job was assisted by the government's intent on emphasising the worst-case outcomes. Data about infections, deaths and hospital admissions were used as means of persuasion, not to inform. Low click-generating headlines like 'Today 99.1% of those contracting Covid recovered' rarely appeared.

Whenever I tried to cheer up friends with this positive news, I could see they thought I was being flippant and uncaring. I think some of them thought I was in denial about what was happening. I kept seeing a look on their face of 'doesn't he get how serious this is?' Everybody knew somebody who knew somebody with a relative who had died or was seriously ill with Covid. This technique of using a particular instance to create a bad news story that is then generalised became a standard ploy of the media (and friends). Not for an instant was I trivialising the pandemic's awful effects, but exposing people to unrelenting gloom caused more problems than it solved.

Isn't it odd that throughout the world wars the news machine was intent on generating positive stories for morale purposes, often blatant propaganda? Yet during the only other global incident in my lifetime, the opposite happened. Towards the end of the book, we will look at the impact this has had on the mental health of the country. It's safe to say that we overdosed on bad news and the results aren't good. It's like the country's collective mental BMI has shot up to 35 and is still rising.

I started to wonder if I was imagining the media's increasing gloominess. Then I discovered that researchers in New Zealand had measured the change in sentiment of publications from 50 media outlets in the US. Over 23 million headlines were analysed for the period 2000–2019, showing them getting steadily grumpier. And this period doesn't include the pandemic.

These two charts show a relentless increase in fearful and angry headlines at the expense of those that were neutral and joyful.

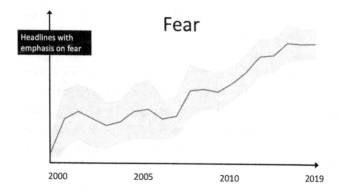

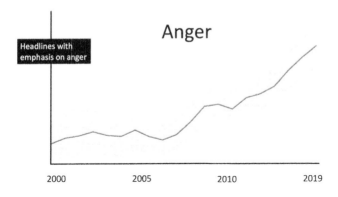

The human self-preservation instinct is strong – stronger than any of the behaviours described in this chapter. Continually being bombarded with doom and gloom, our instincts are screaming 'enough is enough' and telling us to avoid or limit our news intake. The Reuters Institute has been tracking this global reaction, which it calls selective news avoidance, and it's growing fast, especially among women. Approximately 50% of Brits say they have stopped watching or are avoiding the news; it's 40% in the US. Lacking trust in news sources is part of the reason, but the dominant drivers are the feelings of powerlessness and the negative mood it generates.

Nobody has a clue how this conflict between the negativity bias and news avoidance instinct will evolve. My money is on the latter being the winner.

Simple answers

We don't have the time, energy or ability to search for the complete answer to most questions so, instead, we look for the simplest of explanations. When I ask a chum about his recent train journey to London I don't expect to hear (nor am I interested) that the train was ten minutes late departing, the heating was stuck on hot, there was a large noisy party of school children with two teachers who failed to keep them quiet since they were watching videos on their iPads, that it arrived in London on time, with two of the doors stuck closed and the automatic barriers at the station weren't working. Rather, I expect the answer 'as bad as usual', a response that echoes their ingrained dislike of the train company or 'a bit of a pain, but we arrived on time' if they are usually satisfied with the service (though there are fewer people in this latter category).

Very few questions have simple answers, but that is what we instinctively want. A short sharp, black or white (no shades of grey) answer. When in 2016 the UK had a referendum about leaving the EU, 17,410,742 people voted to leave and 16,141,241 to stay. Six years after the vote, the complicated make-up of these two huge groups has been reduced to crude stereotypes – Brexiteers and Remainers. When (if) you ever moan about the result of the referendum, the complex arguments are forgotten. All that is left are the few headline facts that are associated with each group. Do you really think the millions of people on the opposing sides had the same handful of views? That's patent nonsense, but we all share in the make-believe because we need simple reassuring answers that make us feel good.

'Mind-lock'

We do change our minds, but not very often. Once an idea, opinion or piece of knowledge gets lodged in our heads we do our damnedest to keep it there in pristine condition, unsullied by more recent and better quality information. Just think how exhausting life would be if we continually had to form opinions from first principles and make decisions based on the best available evidence.

It's much easier to retrieve a previously reached conclusion and apply it to the new situation. This dependence on pre-packed opinions is called 'anchoring'. I think the term 'mind-lock' is much more evocative of what is happening.

Our unwillingness, or is it an inability?, to process fresh information and change our views should be an embarrassment. But no, we fickle humans have turned this weakness into something to boast about. How often have you heard people claim triumphantly, 'I have always voted for XYZ party' or say 'I have never liked XYZ' or observe 'They always do XYZ.' You might as well say 'I have my prejudices and I am sticking with them; don't confuse me with the facts.'

There is a famous saying that is used to add authority to this idea: 'those who cannot remember the past are condemned to repeat it'. I much prefer the quote that turns the notion on its head: 'what people remember about the past is likely to warp their judgement of the future'.

Of course, there are exceptions. An obvious example is a radical student who was a fanatical Marxist aged 20 and in the space of 30 years becomes chairman of a Conservative Association in a leafy Surrey suburb. Did youthful idealism founder on middle-age realism? Most likely their views were always (and still are) deployed to gain group acceptance. Change the group, change the views. I can think of a few politicians who fit that bill!

Think for a moment about how many of your beliefs and opinions have changed in recent years. What about those of your friends and family? I bet it's not a very long list.

Moaning is the perfect opportunity to recount our 'mind-locked' opinions. We might update and extend them at their periphery, but our core beliefs remain reassuringly unchanged.

Confirmation bias

None of us like being proved wrong. We will do our damnedest to amass evidence to support our beliefs and jump through hoops erecting barriers to exclude facts that undermine them.

The extent to which we defend our opinions may differ, but we all employ techniques to avoid changing our minds. Sometimes called 'belief perseverance' or 'motivated reasoning', it is best known as confirmation bias, which Wikipedia defines as:

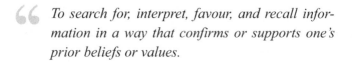

To search for, interpret, favour, and recall information in a way that confirms or supports one's prior beliefs or values.

We view the world through the filter of our 'mind-locked' beliefs, which are reinforced by our selective access to new information. If by mistake we encounter a contrary view, we ignore it or diminish its importance. Can you see the elegant feedback loop this creates?

Being selective about the news we consume strengthens our long-held beliefs and that in turn makes us more determined to reject or ignore information that challenges these opinions. Such an elegant arrangement avoids the chore of thinking anew.

I am writing this section on a Sunday in May 2022. In front of me are four newspapers. Each has a different lead story that reflects its political perspective and values. If you detest the Conservative Party then *The Observer* is full of tales to reinforce that opinion, leading with the headline:

> *'PM to sacrifice top official over Partygate to save himself'* – *Civil service head will carry the can.*

The Sunday Telegraph is renowned for its dislike of the Labour Party and trade unions and has the headline:

> *'Tories in threat to torpedo unions'* – *Conservative ministers planning to break 'stranglehold' on transport and education.*

The content of *The Sunday Times* is governed by its favourite subject at the time, rather than political bias. Recently it has been criticising the NHS, as is reflected in the headline:

> *'NHS covered up ambulance deaths scandal'* – *NHS Trust managers altered files to hide mistakes by staff from coroners and grieving families.*

The *Mail on Sunday* is all about 'shock and awe', hence the capitalised headline. Like *The Sunday Times*, it repeatedly focuses on certain subjects, especially illegal immigration:

'RWANDA ASYLUM PLAN IS WORKING' – *Channel migrants are already asking to be sent home – not to African centres.*

Just given the headlines, you could probably have matched them with the newspapers. That the level of bias in our news media is so great (and obvious) is really scary. Instead of journalists seeing objectivity as their primary aim, many now report the news from the perspective of 'moral clarity', sometimes called 'moral certainty'. They know the world they want to create, and that determines their interpretation of events. That's really, really scary.

I appreciate that Sunday newspapers are very 1960s but all our news sources are biased, be they paper or digital. Even within a single news feed, we, the readers, pay more attention to the stories that support our existing prejudices. We will do our damnedest to confirm our bias.

Before reading this section, you probably believed we are all, well most of us, free-thinking individuals. Now you know we are collections of treasured beliefs that are slavishly protected by news filtering.

To protect our views from critical scrutiny we instinctively select our moaning audience to exclude those who might hold contrary opinions. (There's more about how this can be achieved later in the book.)

The final thing to understand about the workings of your mind is perhaps the hardest to accept.

Short memories

Behavioural scientists discovered that when making decisions, more importance is given to the most recent information we encounter, even if it has less relevance and accuracy than older, harder-to-recall facts. This act of mental gymnastics is called the 'availability heuristic'.

Not only are our long-held views a simplified distillation of the truth, which are guarded using confirmation bias, but they are disproportionately formed by the last thing we encountered that supported them. Perhaps you had mixed feelings about a workmate but recently they annoyed you in some small way. This event is likely to tip your opinion from neutral to negative. Your previous amicable encounters are forgotten.

Sifting through the reams of news stories that flood our consciousness, we mine them for nuggets of supporting commentary that will displace the nuggets we discovered the day before. Over 20 years ago, a couple of American academics discovered a more sinister outcome of this characteristic, which they called a 'reputational cascade' – we know it as 'virtue signalling'. When processing new information, we are more likely to value and agree with those things that enhance our reputation, even if we question their validity.

Recently Black Lives Matter (BLM) became the latest in a long line of events in the history of race relations. I am not equipped to know whether it is more or less important than the others, but I do know it has dominated the debate about race for the past couple of years. The same applies to the way transgender issues have displaced all other questions about sexual equality. Both these subjects have long, complicated histories that have been submerged by recent events.

Being associated with a very visible emblem helps a new idea displace those embedded in our consciousness. Who could have missed the zillions of photos of politicians and celebrities 'taking the knee' (in support of BLM) and being evasive when asked to 'define a woman' (in support of trans-gender rights). The leader of the UK's Labour Party and a prospective Supreme Court judge both floundered in answering this question.

To detractors of this behaviour, it symbolises blatant virtue signalling. There's no doubt that it is an abundant source of new moaning topics.

You might be wondering how we simultaneously avoid changing our views, because of mind-lock, but at the same time are overly influenced by the latest ideas we encounter. It sounds like we are being pulled in different directions simulta-neously. Let me explain.

Our core beliefs, the ones that are mind-locked, don't change. It's the bits of evidence and ideas supporting them that do. Now, this raises one hell of a problem, which I don't intend to discuss, just to describe. Older people have a deeper reservoir of memories that support their beliefs – it's a simple fact of having lived longer. Because the young have fewer memories they are disproportionately influenced by the most recent events, which creates the sort of generational divide we see being played out in the arguments about transgender rights. This subject is worthy of much discussion, but it takes us away from the purpose of this book.

Having digested the red pill and discovered the mecha-nistic way our minds work, you are acquiring new insights into why and how we moan. There's much more to come.

Moaning is a process that enables us to simplify and make sense of our beliefs. Like any activity, the more you practise the better you become, until it becomes reassuringly instinctive. The same applies to verbalising our opinions, which eventually become locked into our minds. Selectively consuming new information protects our fundamental beliefs while allowing us to accumulate more evidence to justify our views. Moaning is the lubrication that keeps our mental short-cuts working effectively.

MOANING AT WARP SPEED

Using social media and messaging apps consumes about half the time we are online. What else, other than sleeping, devours so much of our day? What the hell did we do with all this time before the invention of the smartphone?

The traffic data of social media and messaging companies is incredible:

- Twitter receives 500 million tweets per day.
- Facebook's 3 billion members post 500,000 comments every minute.
- Over a billion YouTube and TikTok videos are watched every day.
- 100 billion messages are sent each day using WhatsApp.
- Snapchat stories are viewed 10 billion times a day.

Is it any wonder that social media is overtaking traditional channels as the source of news, especially among the young? This creates a confusing mishmash of digital media and personal content.

In the previous section, I described how our mechanistic

minds make sense of the world. For generations, these mental processes have been plodding along fuelled by the quaint old communications channels of paper books, TV, newspapers, telephones and face-to-face talking. And then came smartphones, social media and messaging. What mental gymnastics have we employed to cope? What has all this done to the way we moan?

Online and on edge

Professor Jordan Peterson, the clinical psychologist and author, is extremely concerned about the effects of digital media on society. You could say he is traumatised, and that's using the classical, not the inflated, definition of the word. He suggests that mass communication systems are polluting the social world beyond repair and are 'Prima facie insane. And contagiously so.'

A more graphic expression of concern came from a mental health adviser: 'Unrestricted use of social media has been like giving a bottle of vodka to a nine-year-old and saying: "Good luck".' Another commentator identified what they called the 'negative chaos mentality' that pervades so much of the content.

I am not sure I would be so worried, or should I say apocalyptic, although after reading this section you might think I am.

The staggering volume of transactions generated by the digital world provides endless opportunities for shouting our opinions to whoever wants to listen. Newspapers used to be published once a day, the culmination of the daily news cycle. Now, continuously updated 24/7, they produce a stream of push notifications about 'breaking news' of dubious importance. Gone are the days of writing a letter to the editor in the vain hope it would be published. Got something on your mind, then dive into the comments section and tell it to the world. It's a moaner's paradise.

With little effort, we can locate a torrent of commentary that supports our beliefs. We don't even need to think about doing it, because the online applications do it for us. Twitter's 'Trending' feature delivers content based on our interests and location. Updated daily, it allows us to 'discover the hottest emerging topics of discussion'. When Twitter's designers discovered the 'availability heuristic' they must have been overjoyed, exploiting it to drive traffic to their app.

Having access to limitless content and opportunities to express our views has resulted in some unforeseen, unpleasant and dangerous outcomes. Getting attention in this deluge of content means shouting louder. We have already seen how language inflation results in an ugly distortion of meaning, how things no longer rise but 'soar' and that anything unpleasant is always 'toxic'. Clickbait was once a term reserved for writing misleading and sensationalised headlines to lure the reader to click and read. Sadly, it has become fused into how we communicate. It's as if our volume controls are jammed on maximum.

Dialogue conducted online, especially when we are anonymous, is different from face-to-face communications. The language becomes more abrupt and direct as we discard the social norms that govern real-world discourse – let alone the rules of English grammar. With the volume on full blast, we use shock and awe (insults) to get attention. Rational debate is impossible and is replaced by short sentences of denunciation. Too often this includes insults and sometimes threats.

Viewed in moaning terms, communicating online generates spluttering rants, not crafted moans.

This unpleasant behaviour is called the 'online disinhibition effect'. It was first observed when people talked on their mobile phones in public places as if they were encased in an insulated sound bubble. Speaking out loud, about intimate parts of their lives, they seemed oblivious to the resulting 'tut tutting', especially from older people. I am embarrassed to admit finding many of the conversations uplifting, confirming the banality of others' lives compared with my own. I even started counting how often people prefaced comments with 'know-what-I-mean' – the record is 45 in a single conversation.

In the same way as cigarette packets must carry warnings such as 'Caution: Cigarette Smoking May Be Hazardous To Your Health', I think social media apps should have banners explaining the dominance of the few. I bet you didn't know that in 2021 just a quarter of Twitter users contributed 97% of tweets.

The same distortion applies to all social media apps – a few users create most of the noise. The resulting skewing of content, to reflect the minority's views, is even more extreme than these numbers suggest. Over 80% of tweets are replies and retweets, not original posts, further amplifying the views of the minority.

These few, noisy users don't in any way reflect the real-world population. Only 30% are female. Most are in their 20s. This conjures up images of lonely, disaffected, permanently outraged, young men, sitting in their dishevelled bedrooms, chomping through pizzas, spending hour upon hour generating streams of inane tweets. The next time some pundit justifies their opinions by quoting 'research using Twitter', remember this image. And don't forget the bots that pump out computer-generated tweets. These might only represent 5% of Twitter users but they are thought to account for over 20% of US Twitter content.

All this shows it's important to realise that digital content creates a distorted vision of reality. Basing your beliefs on the behaviour of the digital world is like living your life in a hall of distorting mirrors.

Remember, this is the 'reality' where we spend over two hours of each day. With the dominance of the few comes the dominance of a few ideas. A warning for the sensitive reader – this is where the story gets nasty. The events, ideas and beliefs that attract the most attention are those that are negative, generating an empathetic response and depicting events and ideas in highly emotional terms. They are expressed in the new inflated language that contains no grey but is all black and white.

Complex arguments about climate change are distilled into a few headlines about saving the planet from imminent disaster. Celebrities cannot be a mix of good and bad but are saints or sinners. A viewpoint cannot be complex; it must be 'the truth' or evil. And all of this is decided by a small number of people, mostly young men, with the time and obsessive mentality to spend their lives online. Scary.

It's not surprising that what passes for discourse on social media is often described using words like tribal, religious and zealotry. As the centre-ground disappears, you are either 'with us' or 'against us'. You might dismiss these as matters of no consequence, since it's possible to throw the switch and disconnect yourself from the internet. Unfortunately, this polarised atmosphere of doom and gloom increasingly spills over into the real world. Hugo Rifkind, a commentator in *The Times*, writes about apocalypse fatigue:

> *I am tired of the looming apocalypse, and maybe you are too. But which one to pick? There are just so many horsemen thundering towards us. Or at least that's how it feels.*

With social media and messaging increasingly becoming a battleground for the dominance of ideas (perhaps I should say rants), it's not surprising that a lot of people want to mediate its content. Using the word 'mediate' is being too polite; control and censor is what is intended – echoes of Orwell's *1984*?

On Friday 8 January 2021 the management of Twitter announced:

> *After close review of recent Tweets from the @realDonaldTrump account and the context around them – specifically how they are being received and interpreted on and off Twitter – we have permanently suspended the account due to the risk of further incitement of violence.*

Facebook, SnapChat and Instagram made similar

announcements, closely followed by Amazon, Google, Reddit, TikTok and just about every other company involved in social media. If any question polarises opinions, it is 'were they justified taking this action?' – a subject I don't intend to get into here.

What cannot be ignored is that two months before, 74,000,000 Americans had voted for Trump to be president and, in an instant, without recourse to appeal, he was banned from all social media apps – not by the Supreme Court – not by a legislative chamber, but by a handful of Silicon Valley billionaires. The enormity of this precedent cannot be over-stated. The CEOs who run these companies demonstrated the awesome power they possess and are willing to use. Nobody knows all their political affiliations, but I would wager it isn't Republican.

Banning Trump is the most blatant example of corporate censorship but there are numerous others, many related to the silencing of voices questioning various governments' Covid policies. The most famous is the 'de-platforming' (what a dreadful term) of the Great Barrington Declaration, which was supported by a thousand academics and a million signatures. This set a precedent of the US government instructing social media companies to suppress views it opposed. Its right to do this will soon be tested in the US courts.

Most recently in the UK, the journalist Toby Young was horrified to find that PayPal had cancelled his personal and professional accounts for reasons of 'Covid misinformation'. Young's blog, *The Daily Sceptic*, questions the notion that the science about Covid is 'settled'. Remember, until June 2021 Facebook and the other social media platforms automatically deleted all content suggesting Covid-19 was man-made or manufactured. A year later a committee of the US Senate concluded that it was. The science about Covid, or any other topic, is anything but settled. That's something that's implicit in the nature of science.

After a concerted media campaign, PayPal realised the errors of its way and decided the science was, how shall we say, a bit bendy, and the accounts magically came back to life.

Equally concerning is the use of algorithms that scan and reject our commentary if it fails some unknown test. When my parents chose my Christian name (Dick) they could never have dreamt of the hassle it creates with online platforms. Because of the word's association with a certain part of the male anatomy I often receive the message 'your comments might offend and are being considered by our editorial staff'. This is a harmless example, but it makes you wonder what other patterns of characters are thought objectionable.

Governments, not surprisingly, believe it is their role to police the digital world. The US has created the Disinformation Governance Board (ahhhh, another dreadful name) and the UK has recently passed legislation (The Online Harms Bill) enabling the state to decide what is 'harmful' and use the digital equivalent of the censor's red pen.

These ventures are likely to collapse under the weight of their bureaucratic overhead and, in the case of the UK, the chaos resulting from forever changing prime ministers. But, the direction of travel is clear – the state wants more control of online speech. If you know how to determine when information becomes disinformation or misinformation or even malinformation and when truth becomes 'harmful', let me know.

Whoops, I nearly forgot, the EU's commissioner for 'values and transparency' also wants to control digital content using the Digital Services Act and then there is China, the world leader in digital surveillance. Looks like a growth industry for the foreseeable future is digital censorship.

Questions about censorship have got mixed up with the mishmash of identity politics so that when Elon Musk talked about buying Twitter it caused a storm of protest about his supposedly right-wing views. The howls of anguish have increased now he owns the company and has sacked half its staff. Yet when the owners of social media companies act in unison and proudly claim their allegiance to the progressive agenda of the left it isn't viewed in the same partisan light.

All these topics deserve much more discussion, but I will leave that to others. Yes, we have access to unlimited amounts of commentary and outlets to express our opinions, but, and it is a mighty important 'but', it comes at a cost. Not only is our perception of the truth distorted, as is how we think and express ourselves, but increasingly big tech and governments are imposing their bias. All this changes how we moan, and it isn't for the better.

At the close of 2022, when this book was in the production phase, a stream of revelations began tumbling out of Twitter. Elon Musk opened the company's internal documents to a group of journalists. What they found confirmed the suspicion that Twitter and other social media companies were constantly responding to requests from America's host of security services – the FBI and CIA, to name two.

The findings are a treasure trove for moaners.

Banning Trump wasn't done because he incited violence but as a reaction to Twitter's staff, who were howling for his demise. The semantic gymnastics that were performed to find reasons for banning him but allow Iran's Ayatollah Ali Khamenei to tweet that Israel was 'a malignant cancerous tumour in the West Asian region that has to be removed and eradicated' was worthy of an Olympic gold medal.

The censorship apparatus that was used to stop the reporting of the information on President Biden's son's laptop and the academics questioning the official Covid policy would make the KGB and probably the Chinese envious.

When social media becomes a tool of the state, we should all worry and moan!

Pushed to extremes

How have our mental processes coped with this staggering increase in the volume and type of content? There's no single or simple answer since we don't all indulge in this digital wonderland in the same way. No doubt some readers are thinking 'what's the problem with all this social media stuff, it doesn't affect my life?' I beg to differ. If I was writing online (anonymously) I would probably say 'Rubbish', maybe an even more derogatory word. Even if you don't know a Facebook message from a Twitter tweet and prefer the postal services to messaging, you are not immune from the upheaval.

There is something weird and disturbing going on. Only a hermit would be unaware of the terms 'culture wars' and 'cancel culture' and the newfound obsession with the issues of race equity, climate control and sexual diversity. A decade ago you might have occasionally heard of somebody being an 'activist'; now the young see it as an alternative career. In 2017 nobody in the UK's mainstream media used the term 'cancel culture' – by 2021 about 4,000 articles mentioned the term. In the last 20 minutes, 40 tweets on Twitter (UK) referenced it.

A lot of these changes are, in my opinion, by-products of our mental processes being forced to adapt to the torrent of digital content. We have pushed to the limit, and probably beyond, the mechanistic shortcuts that control how we think.

This pressure of digital overload can best be seen in the views of UK undergraduate university students. Research conducted in 2022 by HEPI found 40% of students agree with the statement 'universities are becoming less tolerant of a wide range of viewpoints'. A third of students think that debating an issue makes it acceptable. OK, you need to read the previous sentence a few times to appreciate its importance. Not surprisingly, students overwhelmingly (90%) believe you must accede to those demanding 'safety', whatever that is. No wonder the mental health of students is so bad. If you believe the research from the charity Humen, 57% of students surveyed had used advice services including counselling, helplines, self-help resources and wellbeing groups. The situation in the US is if anything worse, with a quarter of university students taking some form of psychiatric medication.

Our need for simple answers to complex questions has resulted in all the trappings of rational argument disappearing as they morph into tribal narratives expounded with religious ferocity. Expressing our beliefs has gone from 'I think' to 'I know' to 'I'm right' and for some to 'you're evil if you disagree'. Ironically, many of these convictions are about subjects requiring a scientific education that few possess. We have become immune to seeing young people, with a rudimentary education, screaming their beliefs about subjects they cannot possibly understand. Look no further than the reverence given to the statements of a certain Swedish young lady.

Think for a moment how rarely a discourse changes attitudes and beliefs. If anything, opinions become more entrenched. When did you last change your mind about an issue, any issue? There's less and less time to question and reason, so remaining anchored to our beliefs becomes ever more necessary. For some, 'mind-lock' has become a self-constructed 'mind prison'. I haven't got time to consider something that might challenge my beliefs; just give me more evidence that will support and protect the ones I have.

By comparison with the hours spent gazing at their smartphones, Americans spend 17 minutes a day reading a physical book and eight minutes with a newspaper. Receiving so much content on a computer screen has multiple downsides. Rather than processing it all, we scan for keywords, similar to speed reading, sacrificing understanding for speed. We are constantly distracted by the messages and alerts that keep popping up. When writing these words do I really need to know the Test Match score, that I have yet more mail messages to read and the likelihood of it raining in the next five minutes? Worst of all, I am constantly tempted to switch applications to something more interesting, like reading my WhatsApp messages even though I read them two minutes ago.

Is it any surprise that there is a marked deterioration in our attention span and a reduction in our ability to handle complexity? That's one hell of a price to pay for being swamped with content, even if it is marvellous moaning material.

Moaning 24/7

At mealtimes, my parents moaned – not to excess but, as a child, I found it monumentally boring. Children's distaste for adult conversation is one of the few things that never change. The Strouds' understanding of the world came from a morning and evening newspaper, watching the news on the single BBC channel (when our TV worked) and listening to the BBC Light and Home services on the radio. Working six days a week gave my dad few chances to talk with friends and my mum was fully occupied caring for her children. Unlike most households, we had a phone, but that was rarely used because of the expense.

This trundle down memory lane shows how much has changed in a single generation. In post-war Britain, with its dire economic conditions, there was plenty to moan about. However, eggs and meat weren't the only things being rationed – so were opportunities to moan and access to news. When writing these words, I was reminded of how important the BBC was to our lives. Today's youngsters scarcely know it exists. They are in for a nasty shock when they reach adulthood and the licence fee bill drops into their inbox.

Now we have numerous ways to shout our displeasure to the world at any time of the day, about the profound and the trivial. As I am writing this section a court case has concluded between two actors I have faintly heard about – Johnny Depp and Amber Heard. Social and traditional media channels are brimming over with commentary rejoicing at the result (literally) and lamenting it as a catastrophic disaster (literally). There is a smorgasbord of facts and opinions to support views about who was the saint or sinner. Tomorrow there will be another, forgettable headline story to become incensed about and quickly forgotten.

My parents might have read about this type of story on page 8 of the Sunday newspaper. Somehow, I don't think it would have been covered by the BBC news. Now we can select our own news agenda. It's our choice to get submerged in the Johnny and Amber drama. For sure there will be millions of other like-minded souls who are only too happy to join in prolonged moaning about the rights and wrongs of the case.

The spectrum of subjects we can moan about has grown exponentially from ultra-local to global. If I want to complain about my neighbours cutting their lawn at an unsociable hour there is Nextdoor.com, which is used by 20% of UK households. For every comment asking about the competence of a local plumber, there will be two moans about the state of the roads, local pubs, noisy neighbours, dogs barking etc. Local Facebook and WhatsApp groups are full of similar complaints. If you have strong views about the government, there are innumerable places to air your grievances. While you're in the mood, why not say a few words about a couple of global catastrophes? All of this can be done between your first and second cup of coffee of the morning.

When moaning, readers of *The Times* must use their real names, unlike other newspapers that permit nicknames. Those commenting in *The Guardian* tend to use elaborate pseudo-nyms like Fishgirl23, BeautifulBlackBird, Dr Maroon and UnashamedPedant. I am sure this says something profound about the readership, but I am not sure what.

When Barak Obama (@BarackObama) pronounces on Twitter to his 130 million followers we know he is speaking as a past US president. Maybe when he wants to express his real thoughts he is @BarackObama10? Anonymity is perhaps the greatest gift of the digital era. We can say what we want, when we want and not care about the repercussions. Feeling grumpy and annoyed about something (anything), then speak your mind, release the tension, get it 'off your chest'. The inhibitions that stopped you telling friends they are talking complete **** are gone, you can tell @lord_Voldermort10 exactly what you think of their idiotic ideas.

The digital era has not changed all types of moaning. The one-to-one moan with a friend might be interspersed with WhatsApp messages but remains largely unchanged. The same with moaning as a form of small talk. A world full of digital content hasn't created a better icebreaker comment than a moan about the state of the weather. What has changed beyond all recognition is moaning to feel virtuous and, to a lesser extent, ego boosting. All the benefits of accessing and commenting on the infinite supply of digital content allow these two types of moaning to reach new heights and then some. As with all pleasures, they can be taken to extremes and then they become obsessions. The popularity of the 'social media detox' shows that significant numbers of people have reached this state. Wanting to feel virtuous, cementing group membership and pumping up our egos are powerful social forces and being able to do it for free is a mighty big attraction.

I have no idea what the next stage will be in the evolution of moaning. It's hard to believe it can be as extreme as what has happened in the past 20 years, but I wouldn't bet against it.

My comments about all things digital are partly a moan but mainly an attempt to describe how I think it is affecting our behaviour. I hope it didn't read as some technology Luddite pining for the 'good old days' – that wasn't my intention. We can't stop technological evolution (nor should we try), but we must understand how it changes the way we act and above all the way we moan.

MOANING YOUR LIFE AWAY

These brands have something in common and I bet you can guess what it is – Sensodyne toothpaste, RSG Recruitment, Tetley Sunshine Tea, Direct Line Insurance Group, Jack Link's snack bars and SPANA (an animal charity)?

No, they didn't use the same celebrity in their TV adverts and it has nothing to do with where they are headquartered.

In the past decade, all of them commissioned research to quantify how much time Brits spend moaning each year. A total of 11,500 people were questioned, providing a wide range of answers, all measured in days (24 hours). Estimates ranged from two to ten days, and that was just moaning about work; another survey concluded we spend four days grumbling about the weather.

Why on earth would these companies spend their marketing budget quantifying our moaning habits and how come their conclusions are so widely different?

When I was working for a living I commissioned this type of research. It is known as PR research and is a relatively cheap way of promoting a company's name. You commission a market research company to ask members of the public a list of impossible questions they answer using an online questionnaire. Then a smart copywriter takes the results and concocts an amusing press release and with luck it's published by the news-hungry media with a headline like 'Research says XYZ'. You hit the jackpot when it reads 'Shocking news from latest research'.

To boost the chances of success it is essential to have some amusing and controversial findings. For instance, Direct Line Insurance concluded that the 'most moany cities' are Plymouth, Nottingham and Cardiff and that we moan twice as much about the weather as public transport. SPANA, the animal charity, found that 5% of people start moaning the minute they step foot in the office. Another 15% believed they 'whinge all day long'. Sensodyne toothpaste believed that a third of all moans occur on a Monday. Yes, honestly, that's what they published.

These answers are an accurate analysis of the responses given, but that doesn't mean they are 'correct' – how the hell could they be? Asking somebody 'how long do you moan?' is the same as 'how much time do you spend smiling?' – it is impossible to answer with any degree of accuracy. Self-reported research is notoriously inaccurate and (in my opinion) tells us absolutely nothing about moaning habits. In our hearts, I suspect we all realise that these studies are done to entertain rather than inform.

I have searched through academic research for reliable studies measuring moaning time and have drawn a blank. Clearly, the learned academics have better things to do with their time like researching the dog-walking habits of ethnic minorities and understanding why people who eat a lot of fast food become obese.

Sadly, nobody has accurately quantified our moaning habits and I doubt if they ever will. The best we can do is to look for reliable evidence that enables us to make an informed guess.

Back in 2018, a research team analysed 11 billion social media posts to gauge the sentiment they expressed and found that most of them were neutral (85%), with an even split between the negative and positive. Measured over time the trend was for the sentiment to become more miserable and no doubt the pandemic made this even more pronounced.

Another reliable source of research is the UK's Office for National Statistics, which conducts an annual survey measuring 'personal well-being' by questioning a statistically significant sample of Brits about how satisfied they are with their life, how worthwhile it is and their levels of anxiety. Each question is scored from 0 to 10, where 0 is 'not at all' and 10 is 'completely'. The average score for each question is around 7.5 (reasonably happy) and for the level of anxiety 3.5 (reasonably low).

So we have some measure of people's happiness but, as I have said, probably too many times, moaning has nothing to do with unhappiness. Talking therapy might contain a smattering of misery and anxiety, but lubricating conversation and ego boosting should be good fun and are done with a smile, not a grimace.

So we have a few bits of reliable research indicating a reasonably positive outlook for Jo and Jemima Public and we know about the five types of moaning. With this information and your own personal experience, what do you think is the minimum and maximum amount of time spent each day in some moaning activity?

Let me give you a bit more information: each day, on average, we are awake for 16 hours, during which we speak for 4.8 hours and write/message for 1.5 hours. Of those 4.8 hours, do you think we moan for a minimum of 10, 15, 20, 30 minutes? How about the percentage of time spent moaning in all of those emails, texts, WhatsApp messages and other online chatter?

There is no right or wrong answer, but it gives us some sort of measure. My guess is we spend an appreciable amount of time in some form of moaning; but then my friends and I might be unusual. For sure my wife would agree with that statement. I would say the minimum time is 5% and the maximum 10%, which equates to between 15 and 30 minutes of my 4.8 daily hours spent moaning. I asked a few friends for their estimates and one (I will not name them) thought he moaned for at least an hour a day (20%). His wife was certain it was much more.

Accepting my minimum figure means we moan for the equivalent of five days a year – that's a year of our life, two if it's 30 minutes a day. Now you might be thinking, cripes (or some other expletive), I could do much more with this precious time on our planet? My response is, 'If I am going to moan this long, then I should do it as well as possible.'

We have reached a point in the book where the process of moaning has been inspected from all sides. Before improving your moaning skills there is one more thing to be done.

There are three widespread myths about moaners that are nonsense and need dispelling. Men don't moan more than women. The young are just as good at moaning as their grandparents. And there's no link between moaning and being miserable. Let's quickly send these to myth heaven.

- You are spoilt for words in the English language that describe the many variations of moaning. The reason why is unclear, but my bet is it's because humans are instinctive moaners.
- Complaining is an essential driver of human advancement but over time it has been replaced by words associated with emotions and judgements about the moaner. This is a bad thing.
- Our minds have many ingenious ways of coping with the deluge of information they must process. Most of the time this works well but when it goes wrong it can go badly wrong.
- Digital technologies have changed the landscape of moaning beyond belief. Our phones provide 24/7 access to an infinite amount of ever-evolving content. What effect this has had on our mental health is unknown but worrying.
- The amount of our life spent moaning is measured in years. It has consumed at least three years of mine; for you it may be less – or more.

CHAPTER FOUR
WHAT'S AGE AND SEX GOT TO DO WITH IT?

Moaning is associated with lots of assumptions that are downright wrong. A little gentle prodding reveals the connection with anger, age and sex to be nonsense.

· ———— · ◇ · ———— · ·

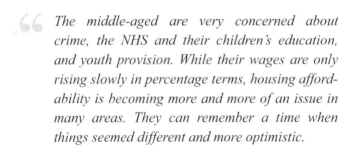

The middle-aged are very concerned about crime, the NHS and their children's education, and youth provision. While their wages are only rising slowly in percentage terms, housing afford-ability is becoming more and more of an issue in many areas. They can remember a time when things seemed different and more optimistic.

These words sound familiar and could be the musings of anybody commenting about the state of the UK in 2022.

What about this extract from *The Guardian* newspaper – heard these sentiments recently?

Continual accentuating of the negative, decrying change and preaching against the evolution of a liberal, multi-cultural society, echoes the concerns of a largely white population which, despite its relative affluence and the realisation of its social aspirations, remains deeply suspicious of modern Britain.

Both quotes were from 2002. The first is taken from research conducted for BBC Radio 4. The second was in response to research that blamed the nation's prevailing mood of grumpiness on the *Daily Mail*. It was written by Roy Greenslade, who we now know was a secret supporter of the IRA and their mainland bombing campaign.

How little has changed in the intervening 20 years, but then you already knew that. In 2002 I was 'middle aged' (just) and was fascinated by the BBC research that claimed men are at their most grumpy at age 35–54. I wasn't feeling particularly miserable, but it got me thinking and sparked my interest in moaning and writing this book.

At the same time, Stuart Prebble, a TV producer and writer, saw the report and it inspired him to create the *Grumpy Old Men* TV series. Thanks to the BBC for unintentionally doing so much to promote the interest of moaning.

The reason I mentioned the Greenslade quote and his unsavoury background is to illustrate the need for exercising caution when reading *The Guardian*, but then you already knew that (I hope). In fairness, you could say the same about all news sources.

I have started the chapter with these quotes to demonstrate how little has changed in the past 20 years and also because they reference the supposed connection between age and moaning. We also need to discuss the gender stereotype. I think Pebble's explanation of this mistake says it all: 'Grumpiness is not related to our age or sex. It's simply a way of looking at the world.'

WE NEED TO TALK ABOUT ANGER

Academics are far more interested in anger than moaning. Google Scholar links to thousands of papers on all aspects of the subject but only a handful about moaning. Search Amazon for books about 'anger management' and you get 20,000 results.

The popularity of the words 'anger' and 'angry' has been increasing since the 1980s, with a huge spurt since 2000.

Maybe it is all the fault of social media? You will always get people nodding their heads in agreement when you blame 'social media' along with the indulged and disgruntled young, so let's stick with that hypothesis.

Wrongly, in my view, 'being angry' is assumed to be part of the moaning process, as are pessimism, depression and unhappiness and the catch-all term 'being miserable'. I have already touched on this nonsense, but since most of the sex and age research references these emotions, I think it requires more explanation.

A moaner can exhibit all these emotions <u>but</u> (double underlined!) it is not a necessary part of moaning. If somebody 'watches their weight' they are not destined to become anorexic. Being worried about the cost of living and job security doesn't inevitably result in depression and mental illness. Covid might have increased the regularity of hand washing but it's not a sign of some compulsive behavioural disorder. So it is with moaning – it doesn't necessarily mean a person is angry, pessimistic or unhappy. They might be, but then they could be happy, optimistic and relaxed.

This is how the OED defines anger:

> *A strong feeling of displeasure, dissatisfaction, or annoyance, generally combined with antagonism or hostility towards a particular cause or object; the state of experiencing such feelings; wrath, rage, fury.*

For sure, moaning has elements of 'displeasure, dissatisfaction and annoyance', but not necessarily 'hostility, wrath, rage and fury'. These words sound more at home describing the latest DC Comics character rather than somebody who is mildly annoyed and moaning about the coffee machine not working.

The reason for anger's popularity and its role as a proxy for moaning is the host of tests and metrics that have emerged to measure its characteristics. These have impressive scientific-sounding names such as the Buss-Durkee Hostility Inventory, Novaco Anger Scale, the Provocation Inventory and the State-Trait Anger Expression Inventory.

Nothing pleases an academic more than being able to quantify something, because it then allows them to look for relationships with other factors and get published in learned journals. Since we can measure a person's blood pressure, let's research how it varies between men and women, the old and the young, the poor and the rich and so on and so on. Assigning a number to something makes it more important and increases its legitimacy. That the number might be nonsense, as I suspect are the measurements of anger, isn't important since nobody can prove you're wrong. Whoopie, we have a metric so let's see what we can do with it.

Let's start with the relationship between anger, pessimism and political affiliation. This topic is attracting much attention as opinions increasingly polarise between left and right. This headline from *The Economist* magazine says it all: 'Why are so many liberals pessimistic about America?' *The Times* asked a similar question about the UK: 'Why are the left more angry than the right?' Arguments used to justify this notion help us understand much of the moaning that dominates the news.

In 1972 a survey began in the US measuring the population's happiness and anger levels, and found that Republicans are always in a better mood than Democrats. Today, Joe Biden's supporters are more likely to have a negative view of the US than those who voted for Donald Trump and, believe me, Donald's supporters are not what you would call 'ecstatic'.

You will have detected my scepticism about this type of research but let's assume it is correct, what reasons do the 'experts' give to explain the finding? You need to remember that most academics are progressive, left of centre with liberal beliefs so beware, these comments are just a little biased.

It seems that certain characteristics of 'the right' protect them from unhappiness and anger:

- Being better at rationalising the status quo than the caring left, who become distressed and angry about racism, inequality and all of the other 21st century concerns.
- Believing people 'get what they deserve', unlike the left, who wrestle with life's uncertainty and unfairness.
- Having more attachments to religion, marriage and traditional values protects them against the rise of secular attitudes and actions.
- Relying less on the government to provide solutions to social problems and hence being less angered by its failure to do so.
- Valuing stability and being resistant to change, which provides coherence to their lives, unlike the

left, who are willing to risk uncertainty and its
associated negative emotions.

These explanations boil down to believing there is a right
and wrong sort of anger and a good and bad attitude to
handling change. This helps us understand so much of the
moaning involved in the 'feeling virtuous' category. How
people reacted to Covid restrictions was a rare time when left
and right responded in a similar way, but for different reasons.
The left vented its anger at those unwilling to accept the
diktats and regulations but ignored them when out demonstrating for social justice. For them, following the rules
became an emblem of being a caring person but joining a
protest march gained even more virtue points. This is certainly
what the 1,000 health professionals thought who signed a
letter saying that BLM demonstrations trumped Covid
worrying about safety.

The right was similarly vocal about rule breakers because
'rules are rules' and there to be obeyed. For them, obeyance
became an emblem of being a good citizen. And wow, didn't
both sides use their moaning disapproval of those questioning
the restrictions to burnish their virtue.

So there we have it, anger and moaning are connected, but
not in some simplistic causal way. This hasn't stopped a lot of
people searching for relationships with other factors, especially how it varies with age and sex, or is it gender?

WHAT'S MOANING GOT TO DO WITH AGE?

For the latter part of my business career, I became something of an expert on ageing. Older people possess lots of wealth and spend lots of money, yet companies ignore them and focus on the young. This seemed extremely daft so I set about explaining why and how businesses could appeal to older consumers. Three books and countless conference presentations later I had become an expert on the subject.

Much is known about ageing. Eyesight and hearing deteriorate, as does skin elasticity. Unless you spend time at the gym your muscle mass declines, as does your flexibility. The list of physiological ageing factors is long and makes depressing reading, so I will skip the detail.

Much to my surprise, I found that companies weren't interested in knowing about these facts, despite them being vital to designing products and services suitable for older bodies. All they wanted to know was what was going on in the head of the older people. Does ageing affect the regularity of changing shopping brands, using technology and spending money? Do the old respond better to adverts with actors of their own age group or idealised versions of themselves 20 years ago? Does advertising containing sentimental messages work better than those stressing value for money?

I tried answering these questions but knew there was little reliable research to substantiate my comments. The assumption that these behaviours are somehow linked to age just wasn't proven. You know the old saying, 'in the land of the blind, the one-eyed man is king' – well it worked for me.

Nature abhors a vacuum so in the absence of hard

evidence the gap is soon filled with myths and stereotypes. Marketers thought that older people were averse to using technology, until it was discovered they were purchasing truckloads of Apple's iPads. Then there was the theory that oldies were 'unwilling to try new experiences', which floundered when the customers for adventure holidays were dominated by – you guessed it – the over-60s.

The idea that ageing is connected to moaning, anger and pessimism suffers from all the same silly ideas. Here are some of the myths that have emerged to explain this idea, which range from the vaguely plausible to the hilarious:

- Realising the grim reaper isn't far off and that many of life's ambitions will go unfulfilled. Walking to the village shop is an effort so getting to the base camp on K2 seems unlikely.
- Increasingly suffering illness, aches and pains and much worse. Spending more and more time with Dr Google searching for 'what are the symptoms of XYZ disease?'
- Feelings of vulnerability that are associated with the previous point. Developing an obsession with checking your will and lasting powers of attorney.
- Friends becoming ill and attending funerals that are constant reminders of one's own mortality. Finding that you know all the words to the hymn *Guide Me O Thou Great Redeemer*.
- Exploiting the tolerance that is afforded to old people being grumpy. Knowing that your grandchildren will forgive you as you grimace

when they opine about the importance of using preferred gender pronouns.

- Frustration caused by all the 'new-fangled technology': 'But why do I need an app (whatever that is) to get money out of my bank account and park my car?'
- Speaking without thinking about the consequences, caused by a declining 'impulse control'. There are many controls that weaken with age – you don't need to know the details – but the one controlling 'impulses' is pure fantasy.

If getting older doesn't result in rising anger, moaning and grumpiness, what, if anything, do we know about their relationship with age? What do you call somebody who isn't angry, doesn't moan and is rarely grumpy? I would say they are saintly and naïve, but a less cynical person would say they are 'happy'. As I have discussed, happiness is big business and has attracted lots of research.

Study after study has come to the same conclusion – that if you plot age against happiness, it is 'U-shaped'. Satisfaction with life and feelings of happiness start high during youth and drop during midlife, recovering from about 50 onwards. The learned professor David Blanchflower studied happiness in 132 countries and kept finding it obeyed the U-shaped curve. I'm not so sure about this relationship but, as you will have guessed by now, I rarely believe unquestioningly anything academics say.

My guess is that the shape of the chart is now looking more like a 'J' than a 'U'. Even before Covid young people were increasingly reporting mental health problems – surprise, surprise – blamed on social media. The effect on adolescents of having their lives put on hold for a couple of years has made matters worse – probably much worse. If the press is to be believed young people at university, about 50% of their age group, are cocooned in safe spaces and protected from microaggressions by trigger warnings. And yet, as we have seen, student unhappiness is at an all-time high.

I am sure the situation is much more complicated, but what seems certain is that older people remain a relatively happy bunch. Reasons why this occurs are pure conjecture. There is the 'positivity effect' that magically depresses bad memories and promotes the good ones. There is the 'freedom effect' of discarding the responsibilities of work, children and caring for parents. In truth, nobody knows the reasons; it just seems to occur.

We have seen enough evidence enabling us to discard the 'grumpy old' assumption. At best it is not proven; at worst it is an inversion of the truth. Now let's tackle the last myth: that men moan more than women.

WHAT'S MOANING GOT TO DO WITH SEX?

What to call this section? Should I use the word sex or gender? What could I say about the 'W' word without causing the rumble of breaking eggshells?

If the Supreme Court judge Ketanji Brown Jackson refuses to define the word 'woman' because 'she isn't a biologist' and the leader of the Labour Party flounders with his answer – what chance do I have?

To avoid getting embroiled in the minefield of sexual identity I'm making the subject of this section ultra-simple: 'do people categorised as female on their birth certificate (let's call them women) moan, in the sense of complain, more or less than those with a tick in the male box (let's call them men)?' Phew, I am glad I have got over that hurdle.

Nobody has done any research to answer this question; however, much time has been spent trying to understand how 'happiness' differs between the sexes. Before 2015 men appeared to be winning in these stakes for an assortment of reasons, none of which I find that convincing. It was thought that women felt a greater sense of isolation after their children left home, compounded by their male partners being more likely to die before they did.

Opponents of this theory pointed out that women are far better at socialising than men and more likely to be honest about their feelings, making the research results nonsense. They also pointed out that men are three times more likely to die by suicide than women – not a sign of being perpetual bundles of fun.

Since 2015 women's happiness has been through a revival, with research showing they appear to outperform men. Amusingly researchers (all men) dispute this finding on the basis of 'do women really mean what they say?' when answering the researchers' questions.

All we can say about who wins the happiness prize is that the results are inconclusive. There is no evidence to support the 'grumpy men' syndrome, but I doubt it will be disappearing anytime soon. Why let the truth spoil a good story?

So ends this chapter that marks a turning point in the book. We have put moaning under the microscope and looked at it from all angles. We know how it's measured and the many ways it's employed. We have seen how myths and stereotypes have distorted our attitudes about its value. We have 'put the record straight' and it's now time to move on.

The remainder of the book is about how we can improve the way we moan and get more emotional benefits from the years of our lives spent putting the world to rights. We start by understanding the different types of moaners and how to determine the one that best fits your behaviour. I should warn you that we are about to enter a 'research-free zone', with the evidence collected from my many years of observing moaners in action.

- Moaning and anger have become fused together. That's wrong. They are connected but not in some simplistic causal way.
- Older people don't moan more than the young – if anything, the opposite is true.
- At the Moaning Olympics men and women could compete on equal terms.

CHAPTER FIVE

WHAT TYPE OF MOANER ARE YOU?

It's show time! Time for you to identify your inner moaning self. Are you a Mega Moaner or a Mood Hoover, a Ranter or a One-Trick Pony? Take your time – it's a big decision.

· ———— · ◇ · ———— ·

o you recognise yourself from these descriptions?

 Older household appreciating rural calm in stand-alone houses within agricultural landscapes.

Pre-family newcomer who has bought value home with space to grow in affordable but pleasant area.

Young person endeavouring to gain employment foothold while renting cheap flat.

If you have a bank account, if you shop online, if you deal with a government agency, the chances are your postcode (zipcode) is being used to slot you into one of 66 demographic categories. Trust me, like it or not, you are being labelled as one of these 'types', using the Mosaic marketing database owned by the company Experian. Yep, that's the same company that determines your credit score and provides data to the police. Worried about big brother coming? He has already arrived and is watching you.

Having a postcode in a posh leafy suburb, where the average property price is in six figures, suggests you will behave differently from somebody eking out an existence in an inner-city hovel. Knowing where you live provides insights about the sort of person you are – well, that's the theory.

How old are you? If you were born between 1997 and 2012 you are part of Generation Z. Perhaps you are a little older and part of Generation Y (1980–1995)? If you are an oldie like me, you will be a Baby Boomer, born 1946–1964. If you are ancient, you will be one of the 'Silent Generation', born 1928–1945. It's hard to imagine anybody being older, but there are a few, known as 'Prehistorics' (1901–1927). Just kidding, they are really called the 'Greatest Generation'.

There are seven of these age groups and you will be in one. I can sense you thinking 'that's pretty obvious but why bother?', which is a mighty smart question. Lots of people think that generations have common traits – for instance, a Gen Z person is supposed to be 'politically progressive' and a 'digital native', to thrive on diversity but as gloomy as hell. According to McKinsey, in the US a quarter of this generation called themselves 'emotionally distressed'; in Europe things are not much better (20%).

Each generation has its own zeitgeist, an impressive word describing the combination of forces that uniquely define their time period. As a Baby Boomer, I supposedly idled my time away in a haze of sex, drugs and rock and roll – if only! Personally, I think this is nonsense; many disagree and are forever talking about Gen Z doing this and Gen Y doing that.

As a species we feel impelled to create groups, give them strange names and slot everybody and everything into one of them. There are four or 13 types of rivers, depending on whom you believe. Dogs come in all shapes and sizes but fit into one of seven groups. The same with moggies – 15 breeds.

Moaning is no different. There are ten types of moaners and you are one of them. Well, it's a bit more complicated than that, as this chapter explains.

THE TEN TYPES

To determine the moaning type that best describes your behaviour I devised a questionnaire that started with a few questions and grew like topsy. That's not unusual with questionnaires, which invariably take on a life of their own.

I spent ages thinking about creating a smartphone app and a dedicated website that readers could use to submit their scores. All very fancy, complicated and expensive. Soon I was looking at a major project with 50–60 questions and pages of explanation. It was consuming as much effort as writing the book. Time to think again.

Then I realised that I wouldn't have the patience to complete my own questionnaire, a clear signal to abandon the idea and find a different way.

Since the beginning of the Covid pandemic, interest in astrology has surged, with over 90% of people knowing their Zodiac star sign and what it reveals, supposedly, about their character. I am a Sagittarian who 'values independence, is a risk-taker with a sharp business mentality'. All very flattering attributes and unfortunately wrong on some counts; however, it gave me an idea for how best to present the moaning types.

I have created a short description, a thumbnail pen sketch, of each type of moaner. Read through them and decide which one or two best fit your behaviour. They are listed in order of moaning severity – starting with 'Reluctant Moaners', who barely count as moaners, through to 'Ranters', who are the most extreme form. As you are making your selection remember these points:

- These descriptions exaggerate how the moaner acts. You are looking for the essential traits, not an exact match.
- You may find it easier to start by excluding those moaning types that don't match your behaviour – then select from those remaining.
- Be honest with yourself. It's your secret – nobody else needs to know your selection.
- Most people moan to lubricate conversation and for talking therapy. Unless these reasons are especially associated with a moaning type I have omitted them from the 'primary reasons to moan' section.
- You might need to go through this process a couple of times before you are certain of your selection.

Perhaps you don't recognise yourself among any of the moaning types. How about getting a close friend to read them to look for a match? If you are still uncertain, then class yourself as an oddity who defies the rules of moaning. More likely you aren't being honest with yourself.

I think it's only fair to tell you which best describes my form of moaning. Most of the time I am your classic 'Live and Let Live' moaner but with the right encouragement can easily become a 'Mega Moaner'. I like to think that I take a balanced view of people and situations, although friends might disagree. My favourite sayings are 'the devil is in the detail' and 'there are two sides to every story' but, in truth, there are some things and people that just bug me. Then the irrational side of my mind takes over, I jettison reason and feel impelled to relieve my feelings by having a full-blast moan. I know it's out of character but I don't care – it's like having an itch and scratching it, you know it does no good but gives some short-term relief. If I am with the right audience and with a few jibes (thank you, Stella, my wife) my mood can easily change to laughter.

Many of my friends have a similar profile, so our moaning complements itself well. The most important thing is that we talk about our moaning behaviour and that helps keep us from tipping into a negative mood – well most of the time – as long as we don't talk about ABC... or KLM... or UVW... and never ever mention XYZ...

Before beginning your selection remember:

- To make the moaning types easier to recognise the descriptions exaggerate how the moaner acts. It's unlikely you will exactly match the behaviour; rather you possess the traits they describe.
- It might be easier to exclude those moaning types that don't match your behaviour, rather than searching for familiar characteristics. Maybe adopt both approaches?
- If you think of the ten types as the primary colours of moaning you might need to combine two of them to produce your behaviour. For instance, like

mixing the prime colours of red and green to get brown.

- Above all, be honest with yourself. You don't need to reveal it to anybody else. Far better to know the truth so you can do something about it (if you want).

Once you have completed your selection, move on to the final part of the chapter to see how you can use this newfound knowledge.

 **Reluctant Moaner** There is no dominant reason why this group moan. Because of their restricted audiences, they are likely to engage in lots of talking therapy probably with some small amount of ego boosting.

These moaners are embarrassed at being called moaners, probably because friends and workmates keep telling them they are. As soon as they start to verbalise a moan, they hear a voice in their head saying: 'for heaven's sake stop moaning' or 'you are not moaning yet again'.

The intensity of their moaning is not that high but, for whatever reasons, they have experienced audiences condemning their behaviour. Most likely a partner or close friend is critical of others moaning and keeps moaning that they should stop. You know the sort of person who is forever saying 'you should look on the bright side' followed by a series of gripes.

Once the label of 'moaner' is hung around your neck, even if it is not deserved, it's difficult to lose.

Maybe they have been told that moaning equates to unhappiness or that it's 'bad for their health'. Perhaps they once became obsessed with a single subject, which triggered the criticism and it still lingers. Undoubtedly, the 24/7 coverage of the Covid pandemic drove some people to obsess and moan endlessly, making conditions difficult for their lockdown partners to cope. The massive rise in post-Covid divorces and domestic abuse are among the unfortunate results of the confinement.

Whatever the reasons there is a mismatch between their natural level of moaning and the tolerance of their audience(s).

Only when they are confident of being among sympathetic, or disinterested, people will they let rip and have a good grumble. Even then it will be followed by 'I shouldn't keep complaining' or 'it's not really a problem' or 'much worse things are going on in the world'. The saying 'this is very much a first-world problem' has disappeared from use with the rise of cultural sensitivity.

Most likely Reluctant Moaners will eventually transition to one of the other moaning groups. Either that or they'll be ultra-careful to select a receptive (accepting) audience. Maybe they will find a new partner and friends who are less averse to their moaning.

Metrics

- **Intensity** – Their moaning intensity is low compared with other types.
- **Pattern** – Since they don't have a wide spectrum of moans they will keep returning to the same subjects.
- **Type** – A mix of personal and generic, with more of the latter.
- **Rational** – Normally they are rational in the formulation of their arguments, with few rants. Because of the criticism they have suffered they are guarded about expressing their feelings.
- **Mood** – They are often anxious people who feel they should be more instinctive and fun. This makes it easy to get them laughing, although it might be manufactured rather than natural.
- **Audiences** – New audiences will be unaware of their feelings and will be surprised when they suddenly start moaning. It appears 'out of character', which results in getting more attention than would normally happen.
- **Notes** – Impossible to predict how their moaning will progress because it is dependent on the reception from their audiences.

·——— ·◇· ——— ·

Detached Grumbler Their primary reason for moaning is to establish group membership. Always worried about saying the wrong thing, they wait for others to moan and then echo their sentiments.

Maybe these moaners are shy and lack confidence. Maybe they fear giving offence and are unsure of how their audience will respond to their moans. This reticence to moan means they chronicle what's happening, adding a personal spin to a conversation. Somebody starts moaning about the crowded buses and their fears of contracting Covid. The Detached Grumbler will agree and then add some further inane detail such as, 'people push and shove' and 'the buses are always dirty'.

Their moans aren't said with any feeling – instead, they are going through the motions of moaning. Rather than disagree with an argument they prefer to remain silent. Unlike the Reluctant Moaner, they aren't embarrassed and don't have any negative views about moaning. The benefits it provides just don't outweigh the effort required and the risk of audience annoyance. You sense there is more they want to say but they're always holding back.

With a few close friends, they will moan for the purpose of talking therapy and feeling virtuous, but this is the exception, not the rule.

Of all the moaning types they are the hardest to know what is going on in their heads.

Metrics

- **Intensity** – Low, although with close friends it might increase.
- **Pattern** – No discernible order to their moaning.
- **Type** – In large groups this will be determined by their audience. With friends, they might be prepared to discuss private matters.
- **Rational** – Reflects the views of the audience.
- **Mood** – Determined by the audience.
- **Audiences** – Multiple social and work-related audiences.
- **Notes** – With age they might become more confident to state their opinions.

 **Social Moaner** The main purpose is to signal group membership, with a secondary reason of feeling virtuous. Most of the time their moaning is simply to lubricate conversations.

This type has many similarities to the Detached Grumbler. Rather than initiating a moan, they prefer to 'go with the flow' of the conversation.

They use moaning to gain social approval and to signal group membership. Their lack of commitment and certainty is reflected in the content of their moans, prefacing their comments with 'as you were saying', 'I couldn't agree more', 'you are absolutely right', then followed by a summary of the other person's moan.

In short, they are the moaner who only moans when it's safe and approved. They will be very aware of using the right language and having the 'right' opinions.

There is no pattern in their moaning since that is determined by those they are with. The only way of guessing their real, rather than reflected, beliefs is by the intensity of their language and change in body language.

Gaining group acceptance, with minimum risk of giving offence, is what drives their behaviour. At work, they rarely speak other than to agree with the majority. Socially, they work hard to stay in the background and go along with what everybody else wants to do. They are the archetypical chameleon of the social pack.

Even their friends wish they would be 'more open' and say what they really think. With age, they might 'loosen up' but their moaning will always remain superficial.

It's possible that the Social Moaner has the traits of the Obsessive Moaner in that they prefer to moan without an audience. It's safer that way and they can 'say' exactly what they want without fear of the repercussions.

Metrics

- **Intensity** – Low.
- **Pattern** – Determined by their audience.
- **Type** – Determined by their audience. Very little personal moaning. Mostly about generic subjects that reflect the group's views.

- **Rational** – Echoes other people's comments. Having the right moan is what is important; convincing arguments are secondary.
- **Mood** – They will follow the mood of the audience.
- **Audiences** – Multiple social and work-related audiences.
- **Notes** – Social acceptance is the dominant motivation. Moaning will always be a means to achieving that end.

 **Live and Let Live** Their moaning is all about feeling virtuous and exercising power. Unlike other types, ego boosting is low on their agenda.

Most of the time they appear to be fair and understanding in their outlook and sensitive to others' opinions – annoyingly so. They like to promote an image of having a balanced view of the world, but lurking beneath this manufactured image, the intensity of their grumbling can equal that of a Mega Moaner.

Their behaviour is frustrating for their audience. Rather than stating what they believe they will respond with statements like 'life is not that simple', 'there are two sides to the story', 'perhaps we need to dig deeper'… Then, out of nowhere, they start moaning. It's like the floodgates are open and the moans come fast and furious.

They want to be seen as being reasonable and enlightened

but often they are deeply frustrated with life, both personal and generic. Their Jekyll and Hyde character can shock audiences who are unaware of this 'flip flop' behaviour. One minute they are sitting on the fence; the next they have erupted into a full-blast moan.

Usually, they are pleasant company, but occasionally their behaviour is not just difficult but also annoying. They want to infer they are good and reasonable, with liberal and progressive views, but the nature of their moaning reveals they are motivated by exercising power and feeling virtuous.

Metrics

- **Intensity** – In bursts, it is as intense as any of the moaning types.
- **Pattern** – No regular pattern. Their mood determines whether they want to be 'Mr Nice Guy' or their more argumentative selves.
- **Type** – Mainly generic. Rarely moan about personal issues.
- **Rational** – Most of the time they want to be seen as balanced and rational, willing to see all sides of an argument, but this disappears once they start moaning. Because they spend so much time projecting this air of reasonableness their moans sound uncharacteristically dogmatic, almost like rants.
- **Mood** – Most of the time their mood is light but once they dive into a moaning spree it's difficult to lighten their feelings.

- **Audiences** – A wide range of audiences but only with a few are they prepared to release the controls and moan.
- **Notes** – They might not change, but it is most likely the intensity of their moaning will increase over time.

**Just One More Thing** Ego boosting and feeling virtuous determine their moaning behaviour. For a sub-group, talking therapy is a major component.

Mostly they refrain from intense moaning, but their pet gripes trigger them into intense bouts when they jump from subject to subject in a well-rehearsed pattern.

Any topic can initiate their prolonged grumbling. One day a conversation about a controversial workmate will open the floodgates, another, it might be about a podcast they found objectionable. Having started they will soon begin on their favourite moans.

There is a sub-group of this type that takes any opportunity to vent their displeasure and immediately appears to feel better for 'getting it off their chest'. For them, moaning is all about talking therapy, it's a way to release their frustrations. What effect this has on their audience is a secondary consideration.

If you were to observe them over a long period, they moan

far less than Mega Moaners but, in short bouts, they equal or exceed them in intensity.

Their unpredictable behaviour isn't confined to their moaning. Some days they seem anxious to chat, others to remain silent. You never know what mood they will be in – full of the joys of spring or deeply serious and brooding.

Their audiences never know what to expect and how to respond. Do they agree with their moans or challenge them? They are difficult people to be around.

Metrics

- **Intensity** – Intense in short bursts.
- **Pattern** – No discernible reason why they start moaning but, once they begin, they are predictable in the sequence of their gripes.
- **Type** – Depends totally on the individual.
- **Rational** – Some pretence at having rational arguments to support their moans but they are mostly unsubstantiated statements of belief.
- **Mood** – Can change from day to day. Sometimes their moaning is laced with laughter, other times they can be difficult to shift from their gloom.
- **Audiences** – Their audiences are limited because of their unpredictable behaviour.
- **Notes** – Over time the trajectory of their moaning will become more intense and frequent.

One-Trick Pony Their primary reasons for moaning are ego boosting and feeling virtuous.

Normally this phrase describes somebody with a 'single talent or area of expertise'. These moaners habitually grumble about the same subjects and have a knack for guiding conversations to their favourite topics. Mostly these are generic subjects – rarely do they talk about personal issues.

A conversation might start about the delays at airport departures, which the One-Trick Pony will immediately relate to their favourite subject of 'climate change', 'lack of investment', 'unlimited immigration' or whatever. Their audience probably sighs as they start listening (yet again) to the diatribe that follows. Maybe they have got to the stage where they intervene with 'not that subject again', perhaps expressed in more forceful language.

Compared with the Just One More Thing type they are more predictable, moaning at a higher intensity and clearly motivated by reasons of ego boosting and feeling virtuous. If in the unlikely case the moan is personal, then it results from some deeply felt hurt they cannot forget.

An extreme form of this moaning type will have the same characteristics as Obsessive Moaners or Ranters, but in most cases it is more controlled and just becomes an irritant to their audience.

Metrics

- **Intensity** – Medium to high.
- **Pattern** – They have an instinctive knack for linking subjects to their favourite gripes.
- **Type** – Nearly always generic topics and nearly always the same ones.
- **Rational** – Very little effort is made to provide the rationale for their arguments. If pressed it sounds dated and contrived.
- **Mood** – Audiences who know them well can easily turn the conversation to laughter by insisting that they 'don't talk about subject XYZ' yet again.
- **Audiences** – People who don't know them well enough to intervene will either avoid their company or forcibly change the subject once they start grumbling about their pet hates.
- **Notes** – Likely to always remain a One-Trick Pony.

 **Mood Hoover** A combination of ego boosting and feeling virtuous. Their main driver is protecting themselves against disappointment.

Google has numerous names and definitions for this type, which mainly reference their behaviour in the work environment. Sometimes known as Energy Vampires or Eeyores they are 'individuals that bring negativity and a host of other bad traits to your team'.

They suck the mood out of others and can contribute to poor morale, creating a toxic blame culture. What is missing from this definition is that most people avoid them like the plague and think they are monumental pains in the posterior.

A Mood Hoover doesn't suddenly change when they leave work; they are just the same in their social life – the little they have.

It is arguable that they are not really moaners – rather they have an instinctive way of framing everything so that it emphasises the negative. You might say 'isn't it great that the trains are so punctual?' They respond 'no, it just attracts more passengers and they become even more crowded'. You change the subject and say, 'great news that the Covid numbers are plunging' and immediately get the retort 'it will not last – the next variant has just been found and we will all be back in lockdown before long'. For every positive response you generate, they can create two negative ones.

It is a mistake to think these people are depressed or pessimistic. Think of it as an extreme form of 'feeling good about yourself' moaning. From their perspective, their negative view of the world is right (many times it might be true) and everybody else is wandering about in a state of optimistic ignorance.

Most people are trying (not very well) to maximise their 'happiness' – not this type of moaner. Certainty about the inevitability of negative outcomes is something they find reassuring – they are never disappointed – and it gives them power.

A new variant has recently emerged known as 'Doom-scrollers'. As the name suggests, they are continually looking for apocalyptic news stories to lob into conversations. Being the first to know about some awful event gives them a buzz.

Metrics

- **Intensity** – Depends on their audience and their willingness to allow them to moan. Without constraints, their moaning would not be intense but continuous.
- **Pattern** – Fixed. They will always look for the negative, worst-case outcome, from any situation.
- **Type** – Equally happy applying their negative perspective to generic and personal subjects.
- **Rational** – Their rationale is wafer-thin. If challenged, they will happily drop the subject and move on to the next topic.
- **Mood** – Rarely get angry. Their mood is light. They don't hold any strong views other than that the worst will happen in all situations.
- **Audiences** – Because of their reputation, their audiences will be limited to those people prepared, or anaesthetised, to tolerate their constant negative comments.
- **Notes** – Nobody wants to identify as a Mood Hoover; rather they believe they aren't carried away with 'all this positive thinking nonsense' and see the world for what it is, a series of challenges and disappointments to be endured.

· ———— · ◇ · ———— ·

Mega Moaner Most of the time ego boosting and feeling virtuous are the reasons they moan. Occasionally, exercising power is added to this list.

This is the stereotype used for the 'grumpy old' film and TV series. Mega Moaners navigate life by adhering to a collection of beliefs about how the world should be. There are no shades of grey. Ideas are either abject nonsense or manifestly right. People are either saints or sinners.

The news and social media are read and sifted for content that substantiates and reinforces their beliefs. Depending on their viewpoint, contradictory evidence is consigned to the digital waste bin as typical of the progressive left or neoliberal right. Most of the time they aren't able or willing to look for the nuances that suggest life isn't as simple as they believe.

Although the popular image of a Mega Moaner is an 'old bloke' – probably white – the young are just as likely to exhibit this moaning behaviour. To them, the world is filled with injustices, and they can moan about every one of them. They would never recognise their obsessions as moaning but as something much more valuable, described using words like 'passionately' and 'committed'.

It's easier to joke with older Mega Moaners about their constant griping. The young are not so happy, seeing the injection of humour as debasing the seriousness of their beliefs.

Mega Moaners are creatures of habit, meaning their moaning is very predictable. Audiences will get a Pavlovian response to their comments that will either trigger a fit of moaning or words of agreement. For instance, if the audience knows they object to music festivals the statement that 'they are only affordable by the upper-middle class' will result in nods and lots of 'haven't I been saying this' type statements. Suggesting they are as popular as ever and a rite of passage for the young unleashes a tirade of complaints with all the arguments they have used before – 'overpriced, overrated, Covid spreading, unhygienic, excuse for drug taking...'

Their predictable behaviour can be used to alter the moaner's mood, with the session ending in either laughter or angry silence. An audience that agrees with the moans can lighten the conversation by stressing the humorous aspects of the subject. An audience that disagrees has the option to change the subject or descend into an argument.

Metrics

- **Intensity** – Regularly exceed the normal level and intensity of moaning. Their audiences have either become tolerant of their behaviour or will do their best to avoid their company.
- **Pattern** – They have a favourite group of moans that will feature in most conversations. Their views are highly predictable, as is the way they link the moaning subjects.
- **Type** – Most likely their moans will be about generic subjects. There might be a few moans about personal issues, but they are unlikely to surface in conversation.

- **Rational** – Their views are well rehearsed and can appear to be objective and well thought through. That they are forcefully expressed adds to their authority. However, cursory questioning reveals they are not so much rational arguments as simple statements of belief that might, or might not, be correct.

- **Mood** – How their mood changes is totally dependent on the audience. It is possible to defuse their anger and introduce laughter, but it can be hard work.

- **Audiences** – They will do their best to select audiences they can moan *with* rather than at. They are not looking to argue so will avoid those with different opinions.

- **Notes** – Over time the quantity of their moaning is likely to rise and the pattern of the subjects they grumble about will narrow. They will increasingly 'take themselves too seriously' as their mood defaults to remain dark, rather than lighten to laughter.

 **Obsessive Moaner** These people are angry with life. Their moaning behaviour is driven by a mixture of ego boosting and feeling virtuous.

When first encountered they can be mistaken for a Mega

Moaner or a Mood Hoover but the extent of their moaning could be much greater. They 'internalise' their moaning, often focusing their thoughts on people who represent the epitome of their grievance.

Sometimes these thoughts become words when they talk to themselves out loud. Shouting at people they disagree with on the TV, radio or phone is a classic example of this behaviour. I am told by friends that certain programmes on the BBC make their TV magnets for flying objects.

Most people occasionally become solitary moaners. With Obsessive Moaners, it's the default.

A tell-tale sign of this type is that they quickly descend into a gloomy mood, rarely laughing at themselves, unless directed by a forceful audience. When they moan to an audience it's intense and repetitive. Even the most understanding of friends have become bored and given up intervening.

They appear to be reasonable and well-informed people, but their moaning can be extreme and repetitive. Rather than having their moan and moving on, they keep returning to embellish their statements.

Metrics

- **Intensity** – At best they would be classified as being 'a bit of a moaner'; at worst as 'not knowing when to shut up'.
- **Pattern** – There is no real pattern to their moaning. Something will trigger them to grumble about a narrow band of subjects that could be forgotten tomorrow.

- **Type** – They can as easily moan about generic as personal subjects. Whatever is going on in their life at the time determines the focus of their moaning.
- **Rational** – Little time and effort are spent extending and confirming their beliefs, which makes their moaning repetitive as the same comments are repeated, word for word.
- **Mood** – They are serious people and rarely laugh at themselves. If they do have an audience, it must work hard to change their mood.
- **Audiences** – For much of the time they are reasonable people, but their obsessive moaning alienates friends. Only their closest friends, if they have any, are prepared to work at maintaining contact.
- **Notes** – Unless they make a determined effort to change, they become a Ranter.

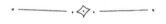

 **Ranter** Ranters moan to give voice to their anger and frustration. Normally this would be classed as talking therapy, but they have long moved beyond that to the point where they don't bother having an audience.

This is the most extreme type of moaner. Once they have begun, they make no pretence of engaging in orderly conversation but instead repeat their grievances in a loud and bombastic way. You might be more familiar with the word 'vent' than 'rant'. If somebody is venting their opinions, it is the same as ranting.

For much of the time their anger is controlled. Once it's triggered their behaviour changes and becomes distinctly odd, verging on unpleasant. When their ranting first started it would be excused with phrases like 'they get very worked-up about things' or 'they have always had a short fuse'. Over time it becomes harder to make any justification for their behaviour.

Because of this obsessive dimension to their character, they rarely have audiences, which reinforces their feelings of alienation.

In most cases, their moans are about personal rather than generic issues. Often, they believe they have been wronged in some way by a friend or workmate. Sometimes the problem originates from within a failed close relationship.

They have long passed the point where their moaning is part of talking therapy. It's possible they have become fixated on a public personality, an event or both. For example, being passionately for or against Covid regulations or fixating on a public figure they believe is incompetent. They are spoilt for choice with this selection.

Arguably, they are not really moaning but obsessing in an unhealthy way that verges on mental illness. Their evolution to this state might have started when they were Obsessive Moaners but most likely they have always had Ranter tendencies.

Metrics

- **Intensity** – Their moaning comes in long intense bursts. For much of the time they score no higher than the other moaning types but once started the intensity can go 'off the scale'.
- **Pattern** – They have a small group of grievances that trigger their moaning. Once started they roam from subject to subject in a disorganised manner.
- **Type** – Feelings of betrayal by friends or workmates are the most likely reasons for their moans.
- **Rational** – It's impossible to know whether there is any substance to their complaints because the supporting arguments are never mentioned; rather, they are just stated as accusations.
- **Mood** – Perhaps a close friend, if they have any, could change their feelings but it's very difficult. Once started they will keep returning to the aggrieving subjects. They get no relief out of airing their complaints – if anything, it darkens their mood.
- **Audiences** – Only a few close friends, who out of sympathy are prepared to tolerate the intensity of their moaning.
- **Notes** – These people are past the point when moaning provides any relief from their feelings of unhappiness. Psychologists would classify them as suffering from obsessive-compulsive disorder (OCD). This condition is often found in young

adults, with between 1 and 3% of the population exhibiting the behaviour.

Well done!!

You have spent 15 or so minutes of your life reading and thinking about the different types of moaners. That's 15 or so minutes longer than 99.999% of the population, which puts you into a unique group. I expect you quickly dismissed the Ranter and the Obsessive Moaner as too extreme and you probably thought the Reluctant Moaner was too 'wishy-washy' and nothing like your decisive and incisive moaning. Nobody, but nobody wants to be classed as a Mood Hoover, yet this is the one type of moaner that everybody recognises and can name somebody who fits the bill.

We naturally take the best possible view of our own behaviour. You don't obsess about pet subjects, never take an irrational viewpoint that no end of contrary evidence will dispel and never bore your audience with monologues about your rightness and the errors of everybody else. We might be tempted to select the types that sound the most reasonable and to, what shall we say, take a 'rose-tinted' view about the way we moan. Perhaps I wasn't being totally honest with you and should include my own weakness for venturing into occasional periods as an Obsessive Moaner.

As I said at the start of this chapter, you might well have traits from several types – that's normal. Being a Mega Moaner, with a dash of Obsessive Moaner or a Just One More

Thing who occasionally Rants… all perfectly natural. Over time you will think again about these moaning types and slowly be a little more honest with yourself.

You know what, I sometimes do moan to myself, maybe I do get fixated about certain gripes, perhaps my mood stays stuck in anger rather than ending in laughter. Maybe I have been misreading my audience's polite silence and maybe they're not actually fascinated with my opinions? It will take time, but I bet you will change your mind and reach a more accurate and self-aware decision. This journey to enlightenment might be speeded up if you get close friends to select the type of moaner they think you are. Do make it clear, they will remain close friends whatever their choice (liar).

So ends the thumbnail descriptions.

Whatever your decision it's time to move on and equip you with the skills to become a professional moaner.

TAKE BACK CONTROL

Let's be serious for a moment. You might dismiss the last few pages as a bit of fun or nonsense. That the moaning types are made-up caricatures and not based on any scientific evidence. I would counter that most of the social sciences and especially psychology hasn't a shred of research to justify many of their pronouncements.

We happily talk about mental conditions like 'being bipolar', suffering from attention-deficit/hyperactivity disorder (ADHD) and dissociative identity disorder (DID) as if they are diagnosable the same way as Covid or measles. That some people suffer from these conditions is not disputed but the spectrum of their severity is observed, not calculated. The dynamics of moaning is no different. Do you really think most self-help books reach their magic formulas for success/happiness/thinness/enlightenment or whatever by 'following the science'?

So, what's the next step now you have been through this selection process? What do you do with these insights into your character?

What's certain to happen is the next time you listen to others moaning you will instinctively try and fit them into a category. It's like learning how physical gestures reveal what somebody is thinking. Once you know the rules of body language you can't help judging those around you. Why are they averting their eyes and folding their arms, what is it they're not telling me? You'll now understand why certain friends and workmates always seem to be holding something back and not saying what they really think. Are they a Detached Grumbler or a Reluctant Moaner? What about the person who always seems to be opining about the same subjects, sounds like a One-Trick Pony? Everybody knows a Mood Hoover so I am sure you're not the exception.

Insights about those you know might make you smile and feel a tad superior but the important thing is you possess much more knowledge about yourself. By reading this far you have thought about your moaning for longer than at any time of your life. Only you will know if you like what you have discovered. You now have the theory and language to understand what before was an instinctive part of communicating.

Back in 2006 a self-help book called *The Secret* sold over 19 million copies and along with the accompanying film grossed over $300 million. The secret of *The Secret* was all about the power of positive thoughts to change your life. Well, it certainly changed the life of the author, Rhonda Byrne. Don't worry, I am not about to descend into some pseudoscientific mumbo jumbo, but will simply state the fact that thinking about your behaviour, in a structured way, enhances your ability to change it – if that's what you want. Perhaps this is what mindfulness is all about. If only I could get beyond page 3 of the teach yourself book I would find out.

My contention is that since moaning is a fundamental component of our character it can be made more effective. That doesn't necessarily mean moaning more or less – but differently. You now have the chance to control your moaning rather than being defined by it. You will begin listening to yourself and wondering 'was that more a rant than a moan?' For sure you will be more conscious of how your audiences react.

We have reached the point of making the intangible tangible. Now let's see how we can improve your moaning – the tips and tricks for using your moaning time better. To make you a thoughtful rather than an instinctive moaner. To make you a truly professional moaner.

- There are ten types of moaners. The Reluctant Moaner hardly moans all. The Ranter's moaning is extreme (and worrying). Each type has distinctive characteristics.
- It's possible you might be a mix of two types.
- Don't rush making a decision – ask a friend what they think.
- Don't take it too seriously; you can always change your mind in the future.

CHAPTER SIX
MOAN LIKE A PROFESSIONAL

With new knowledge comes the ability to adapt. It's time to decide how you want your moaning to evolve. If you are unsure, improve the quality and reduce the quantity – moan less and moan better.

— ⟡ —

James ('Jim') Derrick Slater was a businessman and financier who rose to prominence in the 1970s. Among many things, he was called the godfather of 'asset-stripping'.

One of his books had a lasting effect on my thinking. Called *The Zulu Principle* it related how it's possible to become an expert in a subject by narrowly focusing on one area of study.

His book starts by relating a story about his wife, who was asked to give a talk about Zulus, a subject she knew little about. She spent time studying the subject and soon knew more about Zulus than their friends and those living in their village. Soon her knowledge exceeded that of everybody living in the wider area and before long she had become a real expert. He used this story to illustrate how with a little effort you can quickly differentiate yourself by knowing more than most other people and then use the expertise to your advantage, the topic of this chapter.

That you are now reading Chapter 6 means you know more about moaning than your relatives, friends and work-mates. Compared with them you are an expert, a professional. Let's not be shy – you are a guru.

Slater's reason for acquiring specialised expertise was to make lots of money. Your reason for learning about moaning was a bizarre interest in this oddest of subjects. What do you want to do with your newfound knowledge? Unfortunately, it's unlikely to make you any richer, but you can use it to change why and how you moan.

QUALITY NOT QUANTITY

Over 10 million Brits are members of gyms. Filled with good intentions to 'get fit' and lose weight they slavishly repeat the routines they were shown during their induction session when they joined. Having little to show for their monthly fees, perpetually aching bodies and feelings of inadequacy, many quit after a couple of months when the scales fail to budge.

Those who soldier on fall into a routine of endlessly doing the same set of exercises. If they have a good sweat and leave feeling tired their goal is achieved. They are convinced they are looking more toned and have a couple of kilos of weight loss to boast about.

A few get a personal trainer. The first question they ask is 'what are you trying to achieve?' Increase stamina, endurance, muscle strength or flexibility? Do you want to focus on your 'core', upper or lower body or 'abs'? Forget all this BMI nonsense, what is your target percentage of muscle and fat? Suddenly, this idea of 'getting fit' becomes a lot more complex and interesting.

Most moaners are like regular gym users who have sunk into a pattern of automatic behaviour that provides some pleasure but is done without thinking about the ultimate goals, let alone whether they are being achieved. Thanks to your endurance in reading the last five chapters you can view your moaning in an objective way, stripped of all the baggage that it has accumulated.

In the role of your personal trainer, I have explained the reasons why you might moan and guided you through the different types of moaners. Let's do an equivalent of a fitness test to evaluate how happy you are with its effectiveness in delivering results. Maybe we'll discover that you are satisfied, maybe you need to make changes. My sole aim is to make sure you are thinking about why you are doing things rather than being stuck in a rut. I want you to moan with purpose.

Is it worth the effort?

The March 2022 edition of *Vogue* published an article about moaning that concluded that its purpose is 'for you to feel better, not worse and not to make others feel worse'. Perhaps it could be expressed in more elegant language, but the sentiment is bang on. If we are expending mental energy, getting little for it and risking alienating friends and work-mates, then it's time to reconsider.

Most of us want to bolster our egos and have a sparkling halo with the lovely warm feeling of radiating our virtue. No wonder so much moaning effort goes into satisfying these needs. That's fine and a natural thing to do but have you gone beyond the point of diminishing returns? Are your moans delivering less and less satisfaction? Are you endlessly recycling the same arguments to put the world to rights?

What purpose does it serve to keep grumbling about things you haven't the faintest chance of changing? Don't worry, we all do it but don't kid yourself your insights are original or informed or will do any good other than to make you feel better (maybe). There's a clear distinction between those things you can do something about and those you can't. Generic subjects are nearly all in the latter group. Personal ones might be the same but are often things we can alter but don't want, or are afraid, to.

Let me give you a few examples. Depending on your

viewpoint, in July 2022 the UK suffered or enjoyed a period of very high temperatures. Some people were convinced the heatwave was another step towards climatic catastrophe. Confirmation bias drove them to cherry-pick from the news streams the gloomiest of stories and data proving the imminent arrival of Armageddon. Another group perceived the 'panic' as yet more nonsense from the climate fantasists, supported by risk-obsessed officialdom, issuing infantile 'red warnings' about drinking lots of water and keeping out of the sun. It was a perfect opportunity to moan and moan some more.

I have no idea who won the competition for the most moans but I expect it was a close-run contest. What's for certain is that it did nothing to change the temperature and alter the ingrained attitudes, which almost certainly became reinforced further.

The Covid virus had precious few benefits, but one was to generate lots of new moaning topics about how individuals and institutions reacted to the pandemic. Before December 2019 nobody was moaning about wearing masks (or not), being vaccinated (or not) and the countless restrictions that governed our lives. Very quickly the world divided into those believing 'they' were ruining our lives and those imploring 'them' to be more dictatorial. Heaven knows how much energy was spent moaning about these topics; probably more than enough to compensate for the shortages caused by the Russia–Ukraine conflict. Did it materially change anything? I would guess somewhere between very little and nothing at all.

Some personal moans are ageless. Too much is expected of me – I am paid too little – the work is boring – he/she/they are boring – they want to do X and I want to do Y. We have all been the moaner or audience in these conversations. Gallons of coffee, wine and sack loads of nibbles have been consumed as the moaner and their audience ponder whether they should do A or B or maybe C.

I am a pretty good listener and dispenser of advice but in only a handful of cases was my advice taken. When the roles were reversed, I invariably ignored my audience's opinions unless they agreed with what I had already decided. As I have explained, talking therapy has lots of benefits that are unrelated to the content of what is said. The opportunity to rant (vent) our feelings is beneficial but it's easy to exceed the therapeutic level. Endlessly repeating the same moans, hearing the same advice and ignoring it, does little good and can result in alienating the most tolerant of audiences.

Returning to the analogy of the fitness trainer and the gym user – often their advice is to reduce the total amount of exercise and to do it differently. The same applies to moaning. Before you whinge to the same people about the same thing that you winged about yesterday and the day before, think about whether there is anything better you can do with your time. Mostly you will keep going and recycle your gripe, getting the same recycled response, probably augmented with some snippet of news confirming its truth.

You might want to settle back with your portfolio of moans and not change them – that's fine. But be aware of the risk – especially to your relationship with your audiences. The more you are asking yourself the question 'is it worth the effort?' the more likely the answer will be 'not really.'

Moans are losing their effectiveness

Moans are increasingly truncated, becoming simplistic assertions, accompanied by words of insult. That's a bold claim but that's what seems to be happening.

Instead of saying 'I didn't like the way the film ended' we say 'the film was rubbish'. Rather than observing that 'the football team was without its best player and performed badly', 'they were hopeless'. Rather than providing a reasoned argument in response to a statement you disagree with, it's dismissed as 'well they would say that'.

Nobody is certain why this is happening, but I think the advent of text messaging and Twitter are responsible. Despite the message restriction of 160 characters, young people loved the convenience of 'texting' and it wasn't long before their parents were sending messages between their mobile phones.

Tweeting began in 2006 with an even shorter message size (140 characters). Long sentences, be they eloquent or rambling, were replaced by short pithy statements. The average length of a tweet was just 34 characters, with only 1% of messages using all the available characters.

When tweets were doubled to 280 characters (2017), much to everybody's surprise, they became even shorter. Aversion to using words was affected by the popularity of emojis, images and videos. You know what they say – 'a picture is worth a thousand words'. If you have watched the videos accompanying many tweets you will know that's nonsense.

As moans started to resemble simplistic statements, so their language became more extreme. Nothing is ever 'bad', it is always 'terrible' or 'awful'. What was once 'confused' has become 'chaotic'. Situations are never 'difficult', they are always in a 'crisis'. Once, 'dislike' would suffice but now 'hate' is preferred. As I have said before, it's like being in a noisy restaurant where everybody is forced to talk louder. Shouting is the norm.

Stripping moans of meaning and expressing them with extreme language is most common with those promoting their virtue. Many people find it impossible to moan about politics, economics, global events and social matters without framing them in apocalyptic terms. Politicians they dislike are a 'catastrophe', their economic policies are a 'nightmare' and their social policies are either appealing to the 'woke' left-wing or the right-wing 'culture warriors'.

This extreme language and the highly emotional way opinions are expressed is not normal (or healthy). The American president George Bush enraged many people, mainly Democrats, to the point where their moans became rants. This became known as Bush Derangement Syndrome (BDS). Compared with the ranting that resulted after Brexit and the election of President Trump, those moans about Bush seem mild. Proponents and defenders abandoned all attempts at reasoned moans. Insults replaced arguments and still do.

To be heard above the clamour, moans must become more extreme. Paradoxically this doesn't make them more effective – quite the opposite. The moaner becomes frustrated when their audience's response doesn't match the intensity of their gripes. Only anger and frustration result when the moaner believes the world is going to hell in a handcart because of selfishness and indifference and their audience is unmoved, wanting to change the subject and talk about a programme on Netflix. Worse still, they are manifestly bored.

A recently invented technique to goad the audience into a response is the accusation that 'silence is violence'. All that is achieved by escalating the language is to polarise views even further, leaving little space in the middle.

The predictability of moans is the final factor causing the loss of effectiveness. News sources are no longer selected because of their accuracy and impartiality, but rather for their ingrained bias, another way of saying the things they will moan about. Over a weekend I read five newspapers, the *FT*, *Observer*, *Telegraph*, *Times* and *Mail*. Each views events through a different prism. Before reading an article I have a good idea what moans it will contain. Once upon a time journalists tried to be objective with their reporting. What a quaint notion, much better to be guided by 'moral clarity' that skews the reporting to support the publication's moral beliefs.

Articles in the *FT* and *Observer* will include gripes about the incompetence of the Conservative Party, the Brexit 'disaster' and blaming all the world's ills on 'popularism'. Rarely does the name Trump not appear as a figure of fun or the instigator of some or all the 'catastrophes'. In addition, there will be boilerplate statements supporting the current crop of issues that are important to the university-educated urban classes wanting to feel virtuous. The words 'sustainability', 'equality' and 'diversity' will be liberally (and progressively) sprinkled throughout.

The *Mail* and to a lesser extent the *Telegraph* are a mirror image, with endless complaints about the dangers of the elite's obsession with 'being woke' and how 'cancel culture' is ripping through and ripping up academia. *The Times* is somewhere in the middle.

Perhaps naively I hope by reading all five I might get something approaching a balanced viewpoint.

This predictability of moans occurs in all news content – magazines, podcasts, social media news and most often in Substacks. Moans that surprise us are the most effective. When you know what is coming your eyes glaze over, you yawn and you move on.

My observations about effectiveness apply more to the extreme types of moaners. The Ranter, Obsessive and Mega Moaner are at high risk of sensing their moans are losing their impact, causing feelings of frustration. I hope this is a 'blip' rather than a trend but I fear that in time it might spread to all types of moaners.

Be honest with yourself

Most of us are content to keep plodding along doing the same today as we did yesterday. Change takes effort and can be frightening. It's so easy to see all the dangers of altering some facet of our lives and much harder to envisage the benefits. Don't worry, I am not asking you to radically alter your behaviour, to become vegan or join the Conservative Party, but to think about a few aspects of your moaning that you might prefer to ignore.

By now you have decided your moaning type. Do you want to continue with this pattern of moaning or change? What type of moaner do you want to become? Trying to adopt a different type is extremely difficult. What you can do is think about the metrics of moaning and decide how you want them to change.

- **Intensity** – Reduce or increase how you moan, both intensity and duration?
- **Pattern** – Become less predictable (nobody wants to be more predictable)?
- **Type** – Change the mix of moans between generic and personal?
- **Rational** – Increase or decrease the justification for your moans?
- **Mood** – Avoid becoming angry and introduce more laughter or become more serious?

Hopefully, if I explain why I am trying to make changes to my moaning behaviour it will help explain my suggestions. So far it's a work in progress, but my goal is to reduce both the amount and intensity of my moaning and to introduce more laughter. By doing this I aim to alter the other factors, but not by much. Understanding the reasons why I am doing this is more important than the decision itself.

Increasingly I listen to myself and friends moaning, using anecdotes to justify opinions that date from way back in the past – like half a century. As I start recounting hazy memories of being at university, hitch-hiking around Europe and working for companies that are long since disappeared, a voice in my head is saying 'what relevance are these to the events of today?' Unless we commit a lot of energy to them, our moans get stale and lose relevance.

As I (and others) start holding forth about some complex,

multifaceted subject, the same voice is whispering 'what do you really know about this other than the last article you read in your favourite news media?' There are a few subjects that I am equipped to moan about with something approaching authority but not many and all of them of zero interest to most people. I am increasingly regurgitating old arguments that were once well justified but are now getting threadbare.

The first five minutes of my moaning is usually enjoyable but after that it feels like I am going through some sort of ritual that is becoming less and less satisfying.

Moaning with very good friends, those with very similar views, is still great fun. Laughter isn't far away as we ridicule the antics of our fellows and ourselves. It's moaning with those with slightly differing opinions that is less rewarding. Having to provide justification for my views and statements, which are manifestly correct (to me), seems a waste of time. I know I am not going to change my or their minds, so why bother? Much easier to change the subject to topics where there's more agreement with less risk of the mood changing to boredom or anger. When there's little overlap in our views then best to avoid the subject entirely.

I'm trying to moan less about personal issues. Ironically, as you get older and have more 'conditions' to grumble about the last thing you want to do is recount all the problems. When I ask 'how are things with the XYZ problem?' I often hear 'let's talk about another subject' or 'I'm bored with talking about myself.' So much more fun to ridicule a public figure than to complain about health or family issues.

More and more generic subjects are banned from my conversations because they always result in anger. Don't confuse this with 'self-censorship', which seems the norm among university students and is spreading to the wider population. Nearly two-thirds of Americans say they hold views they are afraid to share in public. That's a scary statistic.

I am old enough to be selective about my moaning. If I think it's going to lower my mood, I change the subject.

You might be blissfully happy with the moaning part of your life. That's great, but at least think about it. Remember that ruts get deeper the longer you stay in them.

Don't take your audiences for granted

Our 'fight or flight' instinct ensures we quickly detect when somebody is becoming angry. There is no such primitive reflex that warns us when our companions are bored or uninterested. We develop this as a learnt skill, with widely differing degrees of success. Being part of a group and listening to somebody holding forth with their lengthy stories is an excruciating experience. Watching the faces of the audience as one by one they disengage. Surely the speaker can see that nobody gives a damn about what they are saying and yet they drone on.

Often the speaker doesn't appreciate that the audience wants a shortish answer to a question like 'did you have a good holiday?' Instead, they must endure a day-by-day account of the weather, the delights and disappointments with the breakfast, lunch and dinner menus and lengthy descriptions of their fellow holidaymakers. That's before describing the trials and tribulations of the journeys there and back. And don't get them started complaining about the bureaucracy associated with Covid.

There is frequently an imbalance between the moaner's

desires and those of the audience. Perhaps it's our natural conceit that we assume everybody shares our interests and is fascinated by our lengthy musings. Here's for some reality therapy – much of the time they aren't. Much of the time they can't wait to change the subject and start moaning themselves. It doesn't take long before the mind wanders when listening to moaners trying to out-moan each other. You think your boss is a fool, you should try working for mine – your neighbours can't be worse than ours, and so on and so on.

All I am asking you to do is think a tad more about your audiences and don't take them for granted. It's as simple as that. Failing to do this certainly makes your moans ineffective – people stop listening. In the worst cases, it can result in horrible ruptures to close relationships. Unreasonable behaviour is one of the grounds for divorce in England and Wales. Drunkenness, financial recklessness, lack of sex and 'constant moaning' are the most common things cited as being 'unreasonable'.

Think for a moment about what you want from your audience. Are you content with a few nods and smiles, with the occasional 'couldn't agree more' and 'you are absolutely right' chucked in to indicate they are still listening? Do you want a more interactive conversation with the audience contributing their own moans that agree with and reinforce your own? My guess is you want the latter, but is this what happens?

Using the terminology of human interactions, the most stable and productive relationship between the moaner and their audience is when it is 'win–win'. Both parties benefit from the interchange in equal measure. The risk is that it becomes a 'zero-sum-game' when the moaner gets the benefit at the expense of the audience, who are left frustrated and bored. In the worst case, it becomes 'lose–lose' if nobody benefits. The moaner becomes even angrier and the audience solemnly vows to avoid future conversations.

There are many ways this fragile balance is upset but nearly always it is because of one or more of the following. You have been warned.

Repetition and excessive detail: There's little upside for your audience when you moan about the same thing in the same way for the umpteenth time. What possible benefits do they get from hearing it yet again? Sometimes the moan is prefaced with a statement recognising the repetition like 'I might have mentioned this before' or 'sorry if I have already told you about XYZ'. This, if anything, makes the behaviour worse since you are signalling that you know they have heard it before and you don't care.

Equally bad is moaning in excessive detail, especially when it's about a subject the audience doesn't understand or want to understand. I must be careful when complaining about problems associated with technology. Being something of a nerd, I can easily dive into a long and complicated gripe about some esoteric technology issue. Good friends let me know by feigning yawns or some other symbol of boredom. The problem comes with new audiences who are more polite. Guarding against this requires being sensitive to how others react, which conveniently brings us on to the next point.

Lack of awareness: When members of your audience start fiddling with their smartphones it's a sure indicator that you have lost their attention. Earlier signs are a faraway look in their eyes as their minds wander and are anywhere other than on your lengthy moan. Their repeated attempts to change subjects are another sign you should shut up.

Reading these few hints is unlikely to improve your sensitivity to others' reactions. What will cause you to change is if you consider, for a few moments, why your audience should be interested in what you are about to recount. Think, am I about to repeat a much-repeated moan that they have heard before? Think, why on earth should they care about the subject I am about to describe in detail? And remember, once they start checking their messages you have lost them.

Dumping your frustrations: You have a long list of moans you want to unload and like it or not your audience is going to hear them. Most likely these are about personal issues but the trend to become incensed about virtue-enhancing topics means they might be generic. Visualise the situation with a group of friends in a pub on a Friday night having a drink. One of the members is visibly upset about something they have read. Perhaps a public figure they detest has done something that has angered them. Rather than matching the pace and mood of the conversation, they want to rant about the issue.

Most likely the group agree with the sentiment but doesn't want to obsess about it and be used as a punchbag, enabling the moaner to work out their frustrations. It's annoying and disrespectful when the moaner disregards the feelings of others and assumes their inflamed feelings take precedence. Mood Hoovers are indifferent to the feelings of others, but then they are negative about all subjects. Audiences either discount their moans or find ways of avoiding them.

After reading this section you might be wondering 'I

thought this guy liked moaning yet I have just read a list of reasons questioning if it is worthwhile. Blimey, he is even talking about reducing the amount of time he moans.' As I have said, my objective is to get you thinking about all the aspects of your moaning, grumbling, complaining, griping or whatever you call it. Once you have self-awareness you can make changes (if you want), as we are about to learn.

MOANING ACTION PLAN

Way back at the start of the book I said:

> *A period of moaning should be empowering and enjoyable. If you end up feeling more in control of life and having spent at least 50% of the time laughing it has been a success. When you or a moaning partner end up feeling more helpless and angrier, then something has gone wrong.*

I am sure these words now mean a great deal more than when you first encountered them. What do you think? Is this how you and your audiences moan or do things need to change?

Before making your decision, there's one more thing needing to be done. So far all the focus has been on your needs and what you want from your moaning. We have ignored the other half of the partnership, your audience(s). Perhaps your partner might have made their unhappiness all too plain and that's the reason you are reading this book? Maybe you have a reputation with friends or at work for being 'a bit of a moaner'? Possibly you have a gut feeling that this what they think even if they haven't said it out loud? It could even be your ventures into online dating aren't going as well as expected and you are searching for an explanation?

I wouldn't presume to advise on how best to talk with your partner. Choosing the right moment and asking a straightforward question is probably the easiest way. Something like, 'do you think I moan too much?' or 'do I keep moaning about the same things?' A more tricky, but probably more important question, is 'do you think I get too serious when I moan?'

It might be that your partner's feelings about moaning are unreasonable. That gives you a problem, but at least you now know it exists. If you want to placate them, use the tools I am about to describe or moan more with other audiences. In the extreme, find a new partner. That takes us back to the online dating conundrum.

Gauging the feelings of friends and workmates is easier and less stressful. Choose the right moment and introduce into the conversation a question like, 'I have been reading a book about moaning and it says that it's good for you.' Don't make the question too personalised or too specific. If they have strong views about your moaning it gives them a chance to respond in an unthreatening way. Friends and workmates who know you well might say, jokingly, 'in which case you must be feeling great'. Those you know less well might answer with a question like 'what made you read a book about moaning?' or simply 'what do you think?' In both cases, this provides the opportunity to talk about moaning. Believe me, if they have strong views on the subject they will grab the opportunity and express their feelings.

udience feedback and all you have read, you

.h your moaning then move on to the next

are a Grade A balanced moaner and suffering

᠁ſ-delusion.

As you are still reading, something about your moaning isn't right and you want to make changes. My guess it's one or all of the following – moan less – moan better – laugh more.

Changing instinctive behaviour is notoriously difficult. 'I must lose weight and get fit' are probably the most uttered words that end in failure (repeatedly). 'I must stop smoking' has been more successful but required the incentives of exorbitant pricing, legally enforced restrictions and advertising campaigns displaying people choking to death. Even so, a quarter of young adults still puff away.

You might be committed to altering some aspect of your life but just thinking it, however sincerely, ain't going to make it happen; you need assistance. I wish I could give you the telephone number of a moaning self-help group that would provide support. Unfortunately, these are yet to be established, although this book might be the catalyst to get them started.

What I can do is provide some simple suggestions that will give the additional support to enable you to change. They use a technique called 'nudging', which was used extensively by governments during the pandemic to 'encourage' people to make the 'right' decisions. In many cases, it was too enthusiastically applied, becoming little more than scare tactics. Don't worry, that's not going to happen in this book.

For each of the ways you want to change your moaning, I suggest ideas to help nudge you towards success. They might appear as light-hearted tricks or gimmicks but I know they work.

Moan less

You have concluded that too much of your time is spent complaining – others call it moaning. I expect you realised this from your audience feedback, a nice way of saying your partner threatened you with a cleaver if you keep moaning (I joke) or friends keep changing the subject when you set forth with an observation about the silliness of something or another (I am not joking). Or maybe it has nothing to do with your audiences and results from feelings that you are moaning too much for little satisfaction.

Whatever the reason, modifying your moaning with partners and very close friends is the hardest to do but there are techniques that can help, all of which require their involvement.

Moaning vouchers: These give permission for you to moan on the subject of your choice. You and your partner (or close friends) agree the number of vouchers allocated and their worth in moaning time. Visualise the situation – it's the end of the day and you are sitting down with your partner, drink in hand (alcoholic or not); the perfect time to start moaning. Beforehand you have agreed on your moaning voucher allocation. Two is too stingy – six is overkill – three or four is a good number to start with.

Strict adherence to the rules is not what's important.

Placing a notional limit on your moans heightens your awareness and provides a non-threatening signal your audience can use to indicate when you have exceeded their tolerance limit (used all your vouchers). My experience is that the moaner, rather than the audience, keeps count as the vouchers are used up.

This simple self-governing mechanism works – believe me; ask my wife. Another benefit is it stops the conversation from becoming too serious. If the audience detects this happening they terminate it by saying 'that's it, you have used all your vouchers'.

Timed moaning: This works in a similar way, but instead of vouchers, you decide on an allocation of time. You can make this as simple or as complex as you like. Maybe morning moaning sessions are shorter than those at the end of the day and weekdays are different from weekends.

Visualise the same end-of-day chat that begins with agreeing on the time limit. Of course, it depends on how long you intend to chat, but ten minutes is a good starting point. As before, your partner, when bored, can terminate the flow of moans with the magic words 'time's up' or 'you're out of time'. Instead of rambling on you know time is precious, encouraging brevity; well that's the theory.

Red flag subjects: Often it is not the amount of time spent moaning that is the problem, but rather the fixation on a single or small group of subjects. From time to time we have all become obsessed with something. Maybe it's our employer, an annoying friend… it can be anything, important or trivial. As interesting as it is to us, our audience might be thoroughly sick and tired of hearing about it. Neither timed moaning nor moaning vouchers can solve this problem. Labelling a topic as a red flag subject is an extreme step because it bans it from all conversations. If it saves the relationship, or retains friendships, then it's worthwhile.

Moaning partners: There's no guarantee that your partner is interested in the topics you most like moaning about. Since you have been together perhaps you have developed a passionate interest in gardening, a subject laden with moaning topics (too little rain, too much rain, the price of plants, roses damaged by aphids etc).

There is only so much manufactured interest a non-gardener can generate about a subject they don't understand or care about. It's stating the obvious but moaning with someone who shares the same interest is much more fun – assuming you are in broad agreement.

The term 'bubble' entered our vocabulary during the pandemic. What seemed a simple concept soon became complicated as politicians couldn't resist messing about with the rules. I want to use the idea in the context of moaning, except they are no longer limited in size. I have moaning bubbles with friends who share my views about politics and social issues and others for discussing sports. For moaning about my interest in the more specialist subjects of technology, music and publishing I have regular Zoom calls with like-minded friends.

As the congruence between moaner and audience increases, so does the enjoyment. You can discard vouchers and time limits and moan to your heart's content, supplementing it with messaging between meetings to extend the pleasure. After another dismal performance of the England cricket team, my phone pings constantly with WhatsApp moans.

Reducing your moaning with larger audiences of friends and workmates is a different and more difficult matter. To some of them you might be able to explain your intentions but for the majority, you must rely on other techniques.

Let's take a step back to remember the reasons most of us moan. It's to generate feelings of superiority and being in control. You can satisfy the same desires in other ways. Taking this option is a radical step but one that I know works.

You now have insights into human behaviour that few of your friends and workmates possess, unless you gave them the book as a Christmas present, something I would strongly encourage you to do. Rather than being anxious to become involved in a conversation that is heading into moaning territory, just listen. Use your silence to classify people into the different moaning types – why are they moaning? – what are they trying to achieve? You are empowered by knowing something they don't. You spend more time observing than moaning but be careful not to become too silent.

It's just like the thrill you get when you first learn the key to body and facial language. In addition to listening to what people say you watch and decode the messages transmitted by their body movements. Standing rigid with crossed arms indicates feelings of discomfort and defensiveness. Twisting the body and hiding the hands signifies a lack of interest, maybe disagreement. Facial expressions, posture and eye contact suddenly take on a new meaning.

In practice you will find the temptation to jump back into the conversation and moan will be too strong – that's to be expected. But, by rebalancing your talk-to-listen ratio you will achieve the same benefits and have more fun along the way.

Moan better

Wanting to 'moan better' is a vague requirement that is unlikely to be achieved by a single remedy, although that doesn't stop people from suggesting them. For instance, *Vogue* magazine says (I have paraphrased):

> *Make a rule that complaining needs to be either funny or constructive – especially when it's about an ongoing situation like work where there may be limited options for change.*

This is reasonable advice and might work with talking therapy but it'll do nothing to help with moaning to boost your ego. Dr Google's suggestions aren't any better, with vague ideas about 'developing a nourishing and positive attitude', 'learning to adapt' and being 'more mindful'. If only it were that simple. The only thing that will result from this advice is hours spent reading a pile of self-help books.

I wish there were some simple technique that when applied would magically enable us to be better moaners; alas there is not. However, there are things that improve the quality of each of the five types of moaning, as this section describes.

Ego boosting: Two factors determine the effectiveness of moaning to bolster your ego. You must be able to suspend reality, travelling to a world where you have the answers to life's intractable problems. And your audience must have similar views or at least be prepared to let yours go unchallenged.

Maybe you are suffering from self-doubt that you really do know best. Ageing sometimes diminishes our confidence as we realise problems are invariably more complex than they first appear. A more likely explanation is your sense of rightness remains undented, but you have lost interest in the subjects you moan about.

At one time there was always a plentiful supply of politicians I would enthusiastically ridicule, explaining the endless faults of their policies. Now I can't be bothered. Not because of their improved behaviour (far from it) but I can't summon up the energy to complain. I know it will do no good and there is an infinite supply of others, equally bad, waiting to take their place.

This is a sure sign of needing new subjects worthy of your ire. What's happening in the US and China is far more interesting and a hell of a lot more important than the political shenanigans in the UK. I still moan about politicians, but not the UK variety.

The first step is to decide on those subjects that have lost their ego-polishing ability. Step two is to decide what replaces them. I expect you already know those that are dreary to discuss, where you struggle to generate a decent moan. Finding replacement subjects might pose more of a challenge although, as I explain in the next chapter, there is no shortage of new topics to get your teeth into.

Your feelings of frustration may have nothing to do with you but result from changes in the views and attitude of your audience. When moaning sessions become more serious, with less laughter, maybe your audience's views have changed. Another possibility you must consider is that you and your repetitive moans are monotonous, annoying or both.

You have two solutions to this problem: change the topics you moan about or find new audiences. I suggest you start with the first solution and see if that works.

Feeling virtuous: Moaning has long been used to demonstrate our beliefs to those we want to impress. This is something of a vague statement, so let me give you some examples. If I want to be seen as a sensitive person who is sympathetic to the injustices suffered by a particular group, then I can spend my time and energy providing practical help. A much easier and more immediate way is to moan vocally about those who are seen as responsible for causing the group's problem.

Raging against an opponent's religious, political, sexual or moral beliefs is much easier than demonstrating support by acts of self-denial and financial sacrifice.

The amplifying power of social media has made this form of moaning more popular and effective. When you see photos of people ranting their displeasure their smartphones are always in evidence capturing the moment and their virtue, soon to appear on Instagram and Facebook.

I am certain that the desire to feel virtuous has been responsible for some of my moaning but, not wanting to embarrass myself, I will spare you the details.

In the past decade, the opportunities to indulge in virtuous moaning have snowballed as the number of causes to support and villains to vilify has exponentially multiplied. Having plentiful things to moan about is terrific but the evolution of this type of moaning concerns me. I sense I am not alone in having this uneasiness.

Anger is an essential ingredient of virtuous moaning; there is no room for laughter. Too often this results in verbal and increasingly physical bullying. As we will see in Chapter 7 (*Moaning in unhappy times*) there are very real dangers when moaning morphs into perpetual anger.

I must admit to having spent time moaning about 'victimhood culture', the term used to describe these developments. With its constant stream of new victims and words to learn it has a comical dimension. Getting to grips with 'mansplaining', 'whitesplaining' and 'straightsplaining' and understanding the many varieties of 'phobics' and 'isms' has its surreal moments.

I don't want to trivialise what is a serious issue. A significant group of people are overdosing on this form of moaning. That is bad for them but worse still it is polarising society as those being castigated as the villains are pushing back and with that comes a form of anti-virtuous moaning.

My guess, and it is only a guess, is that it will be a transitory phase. Being constantly angry is exhausting and can't be maintained. Like Covid, which has mutated into a milder version (at the time of writing at least), I hope the same thing occurs with victimhood moaning.

Unfortunately, I don't think there are any 'quick fixes' to help those wanting to change or reduce their reliance on it. The glib advice would be to 'step back and evaluate what has been achieved (or not)'. To take constructive actions rather than channelling all your energies into negative, confrontational moaning. I write these words more in hope than expectation of them working.

Exercising power: If you indulge in this type of moaning it will eventually affect your relationships. It only works if you win and your audience loses. Not a long-term basis for making friends and influencing people.

Using moaning to exercise power is sustainable in a few cases where the rewards to the compliant audience are significant. When there is no upside for the audience they will eventually disengage. Even the most successful and wealthiest of people are not immune to criticism. Media coverage of Elon Musk (the man behind Tesla and SpaceX) talks about him 'still bitching and moaning about paying taxes', 'moaning about student debt' and 'moaning about Millennials'.

For most mortals, moaning of this type is about always being right. Everybody else thought the pub food was fine – you thought it was average to bad. This use of the moan to signal more refined taste, more knowledge, more experience is just plain boring.

The best advice I can give to those hooked on this behaviour is to take a long hard look at its costs in terms of personal relationships. Was the short-term gain worth alienating audiences? Instead of jumping into the conversation with your judgemental moan, stop and listen to what others are saying. Perhaps you are right, and they are wrong, but what's to be gained by telling everybody?

Lubricating conversation: Casual conversation, idle chatter, small talk, whatever you want to call it, is a necessity of life and moaning is a key component in doing it well. Some have the instinctive knack for chatting away, others find it difficult, even painful.

Practice makes perfect, well it makes it better, but there are a few tips that can immediately help the novice. Never,

ever moan about a contentious subject or one requiring explanation. Whatever you say must be self-evidently correct to the whole audience. Think of it as the diametric opposite of a virtuous moan – it must be trivial and if it results in a smirk or a laugh all the better. You might be lucky and moan about something that has the agreement of all your audience. Get it slightly wrong and the result will be a lull in the conversation or an argument.

Humorous moaning is best left to those with the knack for making people laugh, something few of us have. I still cringe watching somebody who thinks they are a comedian bringing a conversation to a juddering halt with a misjudged joke.

Moans can run out of steam so getting your timing right is vital. For instance, the most common small-talk moan is, as you know by now, about the weather. As I am writing these words the UK's having an uncharacteristically sunny and dry spell, something you would think is to be celebrated; nope. The conversation starts with an open question type of moan, something like 'when will we get some rain again – the ground is parched?'; a response might be 'can you believe they are starting to close the swimming pools?' One more moan about this subject might be appropriate but after that the chances are the audience wants to change the subject. You must be sensitive to the moan reaching the point of fatigue. Either say nothing, or introduce a new moan but don't extend it.

The shorter the moan the better. Nobody wants to hear some tangential anecdote that rambles on. Half a dozen words, no more.

During a small-talk conversation, the aim is to be a cork

floating on the water. Don't try and make waves and don't sink like a stone.

Talking therapy: I started this chapter with the advice from *Vogue* about moaning needing to be either constructive or funny. In the context of talking therapy, this is reasonable advice, although it's easier said than done.

You might be an Obsessive Moaner, the type that doesn't require an audience, but for the rest of us, it's essential, especially when your moans are a form of therapy.

Your audience is likely to be a close friend(s) and the session is arranged not spontaneous. This means you can plan what you want to achieve. It might be to blow off emotional steam, get validation or ask for advice.

Like all good things, complaining has its limits. If all you are doing is voicing the same moans to the same person, then something is wrong. Maybe a very good friend will be frank and say that churning in an endless loop of moaning is self-indulgent and boring for the listener – perhaps not using these words. More likely they will say nothing, but you find their diary is uncharacteristically busy when you next want to meet.

It sounds horribly clinical, but before meeting you should ask yourself 'what do I want to get out of it?' If it is to vent emotional steam and get the relief of verbalising your frustrations, then say so, but limit the moan's duration. If it is to ask for advice, then listen to what's said. If it is to test 'should I do A or B?' then pay attention to the answer. Ask for clarification and amplification but if your response starts with 'yes but' it means you aren't really listening.

Summarising in a single sentence: access to talking

therapy is a benefit of friendship that should be valued and not taken for granted.

This chapter's objective was to help you change why and how you moan. That's assuming that's what you wanted to do. Alas there is no single earth-shattering solution. Instead, there are lots of small ways you can influence your behaviour. Should any of them slip your mind they are all explained in the glossary.

- Moaning can become a ritual. A pleasant ritual, but one that gradually loses its effectiveness. Perhaps it's time for you to change?
- Unless they are continually renewed, moans become stale and boring – even for the moaner.
- Moaners tend to take their audiences for granted. With a couple of exceptions, all moaning types depend on an active and supportive audience. What value do your audiences get when you moan?
- Laughter is a vital component of successful moaning. When it is replaced by anger and frustration, alarm bells should ring.
- You are privileged to have the knowledge and tools to moan less and to moan better. Make sure you use them.

CHAPTER SEVEN
MOANING IN UNHAPPY TIMES

It is all too easy to gorge on gloom, to take the most pessimistic view of life. Never has it been more important to take control of your moaning.

. ——— . ◇ . ——— .

T n May 1997 Tony Blair was elected prime minister with a massive 179-seat majority. The song 'Things can only get better' featured throughout the election campaign and is invariably played during documentaries about those times. It's a lively, happy and immensely annoying tune recorded by D:Ream, a group from Northern Ireland.

When the group played live the keyboard player was Brian Cox, who became a renowned physicist and television presenter, a fact that has absolutely no importance to what I am about to say but might be useful for pub quizzes.

After a quarter of a century things are very different. A fitting anthem for today's times would be 'Things can't get any worse – can they?' As I will soon discuss, I don't think this ultra-pessimism is warranted. However, the real purpose of this chapter is to consider what this unrelenting gloom means to moaners. For sure it generates a limitless number of things to moan about but what, if any, are the dangers it creates?

'WE'RE DOOMED. DOOMED'

This was the catchphrase of Private James Frazer in the TV series *Dad's Army*. I say 'was' but since these programmes have been a constant feature of UK TV for the past half-century, perhaps I should say 'is'.

I cannot remember a time when Frazer's words better described the constant refrain from the UK's media, especially the BBC. According to *The Lancet*, young people certainly think so, with 60% of them agreeing with the statement. If anything, these cries of pessimism are worse in the US. McKinsey, the renowned management consultancy, is something of an expert on Generation Z, those born since 1997, and finds their mental health at rock bottom.

Looming power cuts, rocketing bills, water shortages, failing public services, sky-high taxes, soaring inflation, rising interest rates, shortage of affordable housing and systemic everything (inequality, racism, sexism...) and that's just the UK's problems. Let's not forget the global issues of climate change, rampant 'nationalism', the results of 'neoliberalism', threats of nuclear confrontation and mass economic migration. As I write, Covid and its umpteenth variants have faded into the background but like the sword of Damocles remain suspended above our collective heads. If none of these is enough to raise your adrenaline levels, then there is a constant stream of fake and contrived controversies to rile you to anger.

The severity, order of importance and culprits responsible for these problems depend on your political beliefs. But we can all agree on one thing – they provide a wonderful list of things to moan and fret about.

You can argue this atmosphere of doom is the fault of the neurotic media pumping out clickbait headlines to achieve their Google analytics targets, filling every minute of the 24-hour news cycle. As always, the mind-bending effects of social media are a sitting duck to be portrayed as the villain.

Many blame the victimhood (grievance) culture. In this fragmented society, righteous puritans are pitted against the evil forces in a battle to save the powerless victims. No better example than academia's obsession with protecting its vulnerable students with trigger warnings, safe spaces and cancelling the voices of anybody who might cause offence or a ripple of laughter. Never again will I watch Shakespeare's *A Midsummer Night's Dream* without preparing myself to be shocked by its depiction of 'classism'.

Without question, there are nasty things happening that are making lots of people seriously unhappy. I have my doubts about whether the darkness of the mood is justified, but these statistics suggest lots of people believe it is:

> *By the age of 17, nearly a quarter of young women suffered a mental health disorder. Nearly a third of girls aged 16–18 have self-harmed.*
>
> *One in six British adults and roughly 13% of Americans take antidepressants.*
>
> *In 2020 there were 78 million antidepressant prescriptions dispensed in the UK.*
>
> *The fear of climate change has made 40% of young people hesitant to have children.*

As Covid dragged on throughout 2021 and into 2022 you would expect even worse. Ironically, the outlook may have appeared to improve, as health conditions went unreported, caused by the difficulties accessing primary care (GPs). For a time, moans about the difficulty in seeing a doctor rivalled the weather and dog poo as Britain's most popular gripes.

In the US an advisory group called the US Preventive Services Task Force is proposing doctors screen all adults under 65 for anxiety. Wow, just imagine the magnitude of that task. What about us poor miserable souls who are over 65? Sorry about that, moan over.

Much earlier in the book, I talked about eras having distinctive zeitgeists. Mention the 'swinging sixties' and the 'Woodstock generation' and you conjure up the essence of the time. Of course, this is nonsense, only portraying the mood of an idealised subset of people.

No doubt the feelings of today's era will be captured with a single phrase. Because of the enormity and rarity (hopefully) it will probably be a phrase related to the pandemic, something like 'generation lockdown'. I think a more apt name would be 'the long unhappiness', 'generation crisis' or 'victims ruled'.

My opinion about whether this gloomy mood is justified or not is irrelevant. If enough people think it is, then 'their reality' becomes the reality. This pessimism is infectious and so the unhappiness increases.

Some enterprising market research company (Gallup) spotted the business opportunity in researching unhappiness and created lots of colourful charts depicting its inexorable rise. The UK and US are in the middle of the global rankings of misery. No prizes for guessing the most unhappy country (Afghanistan). How the research was conducted is a mystery.

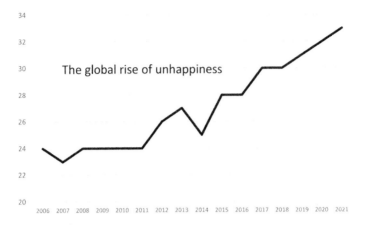

Because the measurement of unhappiness is a recent event, I needed another way of gauging how it had changed over the past century. Being unhappy is one of the conditions of mental illness and so calculating the frequency this term appears in books and journals provides an indirect way of evaluating the nation's mood.

Once again Google's Ngram viewer provided the analysis. The chart it creates tells a story with four clear messages.

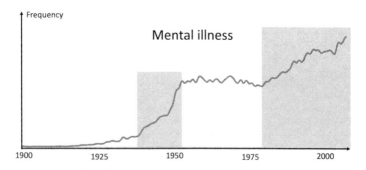

- Mental illness came to life after WWII. That's not surprising since the nation's mental health must have deteriorated, fuelling an appetite to write about it.
- Interest in the subject plateaued between the mid-1950s and mid-1980s. I haven't a clue why. Perhaps we will look back at that period as the golden age of happiness?
- From the mid-80s the graph has only gone in one direction – upwards. Maybe the feelings of unhappiness have been going on longer than we thought?
- There was no upward movement in the graph at the end of WWI. That's easy to explain since the term 'mental illness' hadn't been invented; however, the horrors of that period must have caused widespread mental distress. We hadn't found a name to describe it.

There are lots of reasons to question these statistics. There has never been a clear definition of what the term means. When, for instance, does being justifiably miserable reach the threshold of being a 'mental illness' with very real and distressing symptoms? What constituted 'mental illness' in 1900 is very different from today. Only in the past decade has the subject been freely talked about, something that must distort the numbers. Today, however, validating our unhappiness as a medical condition, warranting medication, may have artificially increased the phrase's use. And, let's not forget the all-powerful pharmaceutical industry, especially in the US, which has an interest in defining mental illness as something best treated by medication.

There are so many things that make this a fuzzy term that resists statistical precision. How the magnitude of today's unhappiness compares with previous eras, especially following two world wars, is unknown and unknowable. However, there is no doubt that the dominant mood today (2023) is somewhere between unhappy and distinctly pissed off.

GORGING ON GLOOM

Moaning is no different from all the other things that make us feel good. In moderation it's enjoyable and beneficial but taken to excess it provides a short-term thrill followed by long-term problems. There have never been more things to complain about, more people anxious to join the moaning frenzy and more channels to express our displeasure.

The detrimental results of too much food and alcohol are

all too apparent. A tape measure around the waist and a blood test reveal the magnitude of the addiction. If only there was a simple test for measuring moaning abuse.

It seems to me that many people who wouldn't normally be labelled as moaners, especially the young, are overdosing on it. Lacking experience they aren't getting any of its positive benefits but are left wallowing in a sea of despair. Their feelings of unhappiness, perhaps depression, are way beyond the scope of this book and my ability to remedy. The best I can do is to detail some of the tell-tale signs that signal when moaning evolves into a serious condition.

Warning signs

Some people have developed a personal brand of being gloomy. I am not sure whether it is intentional or manufactured but it can be extremely effective. One such person is a writer and journalist whom I admire. I was watching him interviewed on the TV, regaling the interviewer with a catalogue of all that's wrong with the world. The programme concluded with him being asked 'surely there are some bright lights in this world of doom?' After a theatrical pause, he replied, 'I think that bike brakes are much improved.' I thought this was amusing (you might not, especially if you have never ridden a bike with rubber brake blocks). Disc brakes are indeed a wonderful invention.

This was a professional in action. He is gloomy about much that is happening, but throughout the interview he and the interviewer were laughing. He never became angry. Yes, it was a serious conversation but it was far from devoid of humour. Increasingly, I watch people espousing their concerns with glum faces and taking themselves so, so seriously. It seems that as soon as somebody becomes an activist they are forbidden to laugh for fear of devaluing their cause.

These are the three behaviours that are associated with this unhealthy malaise – I am sure there are many more.

Doomscrolling: I have already explained how the 'negativity effect' biases the output of news channels and social media to favour stories with pessimistic messages. For some people this is not enough; they scrummage among this unhappy content for those bits that are the most apocalyptic.

People who get satisfaction and feelings of power from being able to deflate positive conversations with their negative interventions (Mood Hoovers) are the most likely doomscrollers. However, all types of moaners are vulnerable to the temptation to search out the worst that is happening in the world.

The pandemic provided the perfect conditions for doomscrolling to thrive. News channels revelled in outdoing each other for the most pessimistic headlines. This unedifying race to the gloomiest bottom became known as 'disaster porn', a term first popularised by the film *2012* (about 9/11). Many would say (including me) that they were aided and abetted by government institutions that always emphasised the worst rather than most likely case. I am sure it was done with the best of intentions, but over time it became institutionalised, turning government information into something approaching propaganda.

Many theories have been advanced to explain the reasons for this addiction to gloomy news. Does it help people cope with feelings of anxiety by providing a distraction? Is it the result of the obsession with staying informed? Is it a form of ultra-ego boosting – being able to out-do others with the gloomiest of headlines? These explanations are reasonable theories, but that's all they are, theories.

I think doomscrolling, social media envy and the fear of missing out are perfectly understandable emotions. If we are honest with ourselves, they are things most of us have indulged in – I know I have.

All that we can do is to avoid descending the slippery slope of despair, to where it becomes habitual. To become conscious of the behaviour in ourselves and others and try and break the habit as early as possible. Otherwise doomscrolling becomes addictive and risks affecting our sanity.

Catastrophising: A role model for those who are always catastrophising is the character from *Dad's Army* mentioned at the start of this section. Whenever there was the slightest mishap, he immediately concluded it would end in disaster. Had Private Frazer been alive today he would have a tattoo proclaiming 'We're doomed. Doomed' on some prominent part of his anatomy.

Why some people race to take an apocalyptic view is a mystery but, as with doomscrolling, there are plenty of theories about why it happens. The most popular is that it's a coping mechanism that protects individuals from disappointment. If you expect the worst to happen and it doesn't then you feel good. Another idea is that it's learnt behaviour from our parents. Like ginger hair, catastrophising might run in the family. Both factors have a ring of truth, but I cannot believe they provide a full explanation.

At school, there were always those who left the exam room claiming they had failed, that they didn't know any of the answers. But when the results time came, they always did well, the swots who got A*s.

My inherent cynicism thinks they enjoyed the sympathy and attention they received after the exams as friends consoled them and then they got an extra buzz out of passing with good grades. They annoyed the hell out of me. I always thought I had done better than the grades I was awarded.

But perhaps they genuinely thought they had done badly and were preparing themselves for failure. If so, they are the obvious candidates for retaining the bleakest view of life when adults, life's natural pessimists and catastrophisers.

I sense the number of people with this desolate outlook is increasing, something that Google confirms. The frequency of the word 'catastrophising' has increased sevenfold since 2000 and it is referenced over 2.5 million times. Something more than 'preparing for failure' is driving this surge.

I have some additional explanations. The condition is a natural outcome of inflating the language, something I have already discussed. Extreme words like 'nightmare', 'crisis', 'emergency' and 'breakdown' are commonplace. The NHS is always on the edge of a precipice and we live in a perpetual state of being 'one minute to midnight' before some awful event occurs. Those trying to remould society, the army of activists, have brilliantly exploited catastrophising by ensuring their messaging is always laced with the most extreme outcomes.

They know that policymakers are terrified of being blamed for catastrophes and the media adores using the word in its headlines.

In the past, sage advice was 'prepare for the worst but

hope for the best'. Today, it is 'prepare for the worst and then some'. As with doomscrolling, all we can do is be aware that the descent into catastrophising is a risk to us all. Try and think again the next time you or a friend jump to the direst of conclusions. Are things really that bad? Are we really living through some sort of polycrisis, or worse still a permacrisis, the Collins Dictionary word of 2022? Might we not just be a tad too pessimistic?

Obsessive outbursts: For most types of moaners, these doom-laden times mark a golden age. For some, they represent a danger. Those at the highest risk of being overcome by the torrent of things to complain about are Obsessive and Mega Moaners. Ironically, the other group at risk are those who moan the least because they lack the coping mechanisms to survive these miserable times. Without a life jacket, the novice swimmer flounders, unable to keep afloat, quickly tires and sinks. Inexperienced moaners drown, not in water, but in pessimistic thoughts.

I first noticed this problem when reading a paper written by a respected authority on investing. As usual, the logic was impeccable, the conclusions well-argued, but without warning it descended into a rant. It was as if somebody else, a very angry somebody else, had taken over the writing. It probably doesn't surprise you, but Donald John Trump was the subject of this outburst. The writer accused him of being among the worst of the world's authoritarians, the equal of Vladimir Putin. Those who voted for him were branded gullible and poorly educated (the 'deplorables'). In the space of a couple of sentences, the writer had gone from being rational to ranting.

Irrespective of your views on the ex-president, this is not healthy behaviour.

In Chapter 6 (*Moan like a professional*) I talked about derangement syndrome – the way that certain subjects cause their proponents and defenders to abandon all attempts at reasoned arguments, instead relying on spouting unsubstantiated insults. In the US the subjects most associated with this syndrome are all US presidents and Elon Musk. The 'two Bs', Brexit and Boris (Johnson), are the UK's domestic issues that result in irrational ranting.

I suspect these bouts of abandoning coherent thought are more widespread than those targeted at former US presidents and their British equivalents. The notoriety of the subjects gives them visibility, but the syndrome is becoming a dangerous part of the new normality. It's as if the barrier between the obsessive thoughts that bubble away in us all suddenly ruptures and they come crashing through into our consciousness.

Of the three 'warning signals' discussed in this section, this is the one that concerns me the most. First, because I have no idea why it's happening, though Covid and gloom overload must be partly to blame. That it metastasises and replaces more and more of the sufferer's rational thinking capacity genuinely concerns me.

In its early stages, these occasional outbursts do little other than devalue what the person is saying. It's when obsessing about the same subjects and abandoning rational arguments become a regular part of their dialogue that the alarm bells start ringing. When they assume their extreme worldview is the norm and to question them is not only wrong but supporting their imagined enemies, you know things are very wrong. Take for example these words that started an article in the *FT* newspaper.

> *Neoliberal policy has fostered grotesque inequality, fuelled the rise of populist demagogues, exacerbated racial disparities and hamstrung our ability to deal with crises like climate change.*

This is a statement of beliefs and no doubt one increasingly shared by *FT* readers. However, no attempt was made to justify any of these claims; it is assumed they are self-evident. They may be true, or they may not. Immediately the author's authority is trashed since you know what follows will be more of the same, rants not justified moans. Like the 'word salads' of cosy terms that politicians think substitute for reasoned arguments, ever more news content is devalued.

I began this chapter by discussing the increase in mental illness and why it's such a slippery subject to define. Whether these conditions merit being labelled a illness is something others must decide. There is no doubt some of them start by having the same characteristics as moaning but can quickly cross the line and become abnormal behaviour.

I am in no doubt that the benefit of moaning in unhappy times, with its surfeit of gloomy subjects, is outweighed by the dangers it presents, not just for seasoned moaners but for everybody.

If only I possessed an elixir that transforms gloom into happiness. Unfortunately, I don't, but I do know that as the quotient of laughter to anger increases good things occur. This has always been the case but especially during these unhappy times.

Fight back the gloom

Walking in the countryside is great for people-watching. Some are smiling, exchanging a 'good morning', others look distinctly unhappy and either ignore you or respond with a muted grunt. It is the same watching fellow drivers' faces in slow-moving traffic; some smile, others look angry. These scowling faces shouldn't be confused with the 'perma frown' that results from inherited genes or gazing too long at a computer screen. A dose of Botox (so I am told) is a rapid cure.

No, the miserable faces I am talking about are just plain angry.

Laughter's importance is not an original thought. It's no accident that the proverb 'laughter is the best medicine' is so often quoted. A much better one is 'what soap is to the body, laughter is to the soul'. My fear is these positive sayings are losing the battle and 'that's no laughing matter' is emerging victorious.

Writing this book has convinced me about laughter's importance in the recipe for successful moaning. During these unhappy times it's more important than ever. I am not talking about manufactured or hysterical laughter but when it is a genuine expression of being amused, of being happy.

The Mayo Clinic published an article (*Stress relief from laughter? It's no joke*) that listed the medical benefits resulting from laughter. Apparently, it stimulates the release of 'neuropeptides' – the more of these you have the better – and does wonders for the immune system. There wasn't much advice about how you boost your merriment other than surrounding yourself with mementoes that make you chuckle, joining a laughter yoga group and topping up your list of funny jokes. Maybe these ideas work, certainly the laughter yoga group sounds fun, but I have my doubts.

Many chapters back we looked at the association between moaning and being grumpy. The two are not synonymous but they can easily become so. Moaning is good for our souls, but it makes us vulnerable to becoming angry, especially during these gloomy days. This chapter therefore concludes with some tips for avoiding that trap.

A good starting point is to introduce the language of moaning into your conversations. Remember, having read this far you are a moaning expert compared with your audiences. Beginning conversations with 'OK, I am going to have a moan about XYZ' or 'what shall we moan about today?' sends clear signals this is an intended part of the discourse. Not only does this tell your audience what you are doing, it gives them the ability to call a halt with 'OK, you've had your moan, let's move on.'

Make time in your busy lives for events where the sole purpose (other than having a good time and probably too much alcohol) is to moan. I have an annual 'Moanathon' when I walk in the countryside with close friends and engage in unrelenting blissful moaning. We agree on the subjects in advance and discuss them in a systematic way. We won't solve any problems but come back physically and mentally refreshed. A friend has a monthly breakfast with chums when they put the world to rights, called the 'fat boys' moaning club'. Since the only menu option is the full English breakfast, it should have a health warning for its high calorie content.

In the previous chapter, I explained the idea of 'red alerts'. If the moaner is in danger of becoming angry then you can stop them by triggering the alert with 'enough of this subject, let's move on'. Subjects that polarise opinions – there is a lengthening list of these – should be excluded from the conversation by putting them into the 'sandbox', the list of topics that aren't discussed.

Laughter drains out of the moan when it moulders on. Having the confidence to take control before that happens and guide it onto jollier subjects prevents it from happening.

You must treat moaning as a therapeutic activity, not as an uncontrolled emotional outpouring. Having the language and being prepared to use it is the best safeguard to stop becoming doom-struck. It's all about applying techniques that put you and your audience in control of the anger–laughter controls.

You might say that some subjects are too serious and devoid of amusement. That's undoubtedly true, but many of those who are professing their anger and rage are easy targets for ridicule. It's difficult to extract many smiles when discussing climate change; however, the antics of some of the more extreme eco-activists have their amusing side, as do politicians contorting their beliefs to appear 'green'. The same can be said for all the other causes that periodically grab the headlines. Serious subjects do have their funny sides.

Personally, I have concluded that I am powerless to influence any of the global generic issues that consume so much moaning time. Using the word of the moment – I don't possess 'agency'. Becoming angrier doesn't make any difference other than amplifying feelings of frustration. Far better to moan about these peripheral events.

Be warned, voicing these views might result in accusations of being cynical, uncaring, obtuse and far less flattering names.

If none of these techniques works you need to employ the 'pull the plug' solution and reduce the oxygen that fuels the fires of unhappiness. We know that news reporting and social media are driven by negativity so ration your exposure. Hard to do but not impossible.

The moaning imagery you need to develop is of yourself luxuriating in a warm bath, continually being filled with content that feeds your confirmation bias, not angrily floundering about in a choppy pond of misery. Doesn't this sound more fun than an hour of laughter yoga?

- The metrics measuring happiness and mental health are all going in the wrong direction. We live in unhappy times.
- The neurotic media's clickbait headlines, the corrosive effects of social media and of course Covid are all potential culprits for this pervading doom and gloom atmosphere.
- Doomscrolling, catastrophising and derangement syndrome are the obvious signs of danger when moaning becomes depression and far worse.
- There are techniques to fight back the gloom. All involve taking control of the moaning process, stopping anger before it starts and laughing a lot more.

CHAPTER EIGHT
AND FINALLY

We have finished our journey to explore the exquisite art of moaning. The final thing is to explain why it began and who made it possible.

. —————— . ◇ . —————— .

sn't it infuriating when authors begin their book with page after page about themselves – their potted life history, why they wrote the book, why you should read it and a long list of acknowledgements, starting with their nursery carer and ending with their doting grandmother.

You, probably like me, want to fast forward to what looks like the meat of the book, but in the back of your mind is the tiniest uncertainty that you missed something important. But, as Mr Bennett in Jane Austen's *Pride and Prejudice* said: 'It'll pass, and no doubt more quickly than it should.'

I didn't want to make the same mistake and with some encouragement from my editor decided to put this material at the end. Hopefully, if you are still reading after seven chapters, it will make more sense.

WHO IS DICK STROUD?

My website dickstroud.com contains all you might want to know about me and the books I have written. Yet more stuff is available on joyofmoaning.co.uk. But if all you want are the top-line facts:

- Edging closer to 75 than 70.
- All the usual academic credentials.
- Once knew a lot about marketing and the internet.
- Still knows something about marketing and demographics.
- Knows a lot about the history of secondary education (yes really).

- Just scraped a pass at 'O' Level English (I hear you saying 'that explains a lot').

What on earth possessed somebody with this background to write a book about moaning? The perfect introduction to the next section.

WHY I WROTE THE BOOK

Was it for fame and fortune? You must be joking. Was it an altruistic attempt to help my fellows navigate these troubled times? Nope, although I would like to say yes. I never got the hang of altruism. In all honesty, it's not until finishing the book that I had a good explanation.

When I began it was clear that my friends were, what shall we say, bewildered by my motives. The first question was always 'what's it called?' After I answered *The Joy of Moaning* there was usually a short silence, a baffled look and a response something like 'that's interesting', said in a tone conveying bemusement not interest. Close friends dispensed with the niceties, looked quizzical and said, laughing, 'what the hell made you do that?' I'll not repeat my wife's comments. If published, they would contain a lot of ****s.

I felt impelled to justify myself and pointed out that they all moan a lot, some more than me, about everything from their relatives to how the country is going to the dogs. Didn't they think it's weird that a part of their life that consumes so much time is little understood?

More puzzled looks, so I continued with my well-rehearsed monologue.

And why is moaning always associated with men and seen as an inevitability of ageing like baldness and the frequency of visiting the toilet? Well into my stride, I continued, are you telling me that women don't moan? And as for the young, they are addicted to social media, spending their life plodding around in a cesspit of moans, rants and much worse.

By now, a mixture of politeness and boredom moved the conversation onto questions about 'when will it be published?' and 'what will you write next?' But I hadn't finished, explaining that moaning has been stigmatised as an unpleasant human frailty, yet we spend an appreciable amount of our life – measured in years – moaning, complaining, grumbling, griping, carping, whining and whinging. They could take no more and changed the conversation to the state of the weather and questions about where I was next going on holiday.

All these comments only partially explained why I was writing the book. Other reasons emerged as the chapter count increased. I adore dispelling accepted wisdom, so what if I could show that all the negative notions about moaning are wrong? What if it's an essential part of human nature and as impossible to suppress as sneezing? Why are there countless books to improve sleep, happiness, relationships and mindfulness and not one about the art and science of moaning? Why isn't it taught in schools? Why can't you take a GCSE in moaning?

Having read the book, you now understand these issues and share my frustration that others don't 'get it'. In short, writing the book was done to rehabilitate moaning so it can take its rightful place in the hierarchy of positive human emotions.

There are other personal, you might say, selfish reasons. It has given me an opportunity to have a monumental moan – perhaps you have noticed? My previous books have all been serious research-based textbooks and I wanted the challenge of writing in a very different style, which I hope has made you smile and think in equal measure. Finally, it was great fun and, as you know, moaning needs to be balanced with lots of laughter.

IS IT FOR REAL?

Amazon assigns *The Joy of Moaning* to the 'self-help' genre of books, a rapidly growing category that has benefited from the boredom of lockdowns, Covid anxiety and the malaise gripping the Western World.

Worth over $10 billion a year, this is big business. The most famous and enduring title is *How to Stop Worrying and Start Living*. First published in 1936, that sold 30 million copies and bestowed fame and fortune on its author (Dale Carnegie). Not bad for an ex-salesman and failed actor.

Today, most of these books are written by third-hand members of the royal family, 'personalities' and enthusiastic amateurs, dressed up as experts. I have spent days constructing my genealogical charts and discovered my ancestors were mainly farm workers (serfs) – not a hint of royal blood. Sadly, the only people who recognise me in the street are my wife and a few close friends. This puts me in the category of an enthusiastic amateur, but not an expert.

I have lots of qualifications, but none vaguely related to human behaviour. A reasonable understanding of quantum

physics and international finance isn't much help in distinguishing a rant from a moan. Pushed to justify my right to
pontificate about moaning I would say decades of practice and
addiction to 'people watching'. I'm the proud possessor of a
first-class degree in complaining from the University of Life.
Don't get me wrong, this is not an excuse but a fact. And yet,
despite having bags of self-confidence I had nagging doubts
about my right to pronounce about the fineries of moaning. A
voice kept whispering 'what gives you the authority to say
that?' Not being able to claim the tag of 'expert' concerned
me.

My apprehension evaporated once I began reading the top-
selling self-help books and academic papers about human
behaviour. I discovered the word 'expert' is much overused
and of dubious value. The 'credentialled expert' usually had a
doctorate in some obscure subject, maybe even the title of
professor, empowering them to pronounce on subjects only
vaguely linked to their academic education.

Other types of experts had discovered a simple magical
formula for losing weight, being happier, making friends,
folding knickers or whatever. Their skill was to take the
insights that filled a page and expand them into a book. These
are marvels of repetition. Rarely was the author a real expert
with the knowledge and first-hand experience to prove it. I felt
a lot better.

That there are no other moaning experts, says something.
Exactly what, I am not sure. What I do know is that in the land
of the blind, the one-eyed man is king. Since I haven't any
royal blood, I will settle for being titled an expert.

DISCLAIMER AND APOLOGIES

God forbid these are trigger warnings, rather a mix of apologies and disclaimers.

If you confused the book with another written by Alex Comfort (*The Joy of Sex*) and thought it was a sequel you have been disappointed and frustrated. Don't despair; the first five pages of Google reference nothing but the other, audible variety of moaning.

I talked about lots of subjects in a way that could be interpreted as flippant. The sight of dog poo on the pavement, fear of climate change and the economic ills facing the poor, all are real and serious issues. That I used them as examples of moaning doesn't negate their importance, but they cannot be 'off limits' for discussion. That they come to dominate some people's lives truly concerns me.

Whenever I mentioned 'mental health' I knew I was venturing into an area that I am not equipped to discuss and, for many, it's an acute if not fatal condition. One way or another it touches the lives of far too many people. The UK's health service (NHS) gets over 4 million annual referrals for conditions such as anxiety and depression and a quarter of these are children and teenagers.

This book is not intended for people with these conditions. With waiting times to see an NHS therapist exceeding five months many people will read self-help. *The Joy of Moaning* is not for them.

Any discussion of moaning cannot help bouncing against the boundaries of what is included in the term 'mental health'. That these conditions are so poorly defined and forever changing makes it difficult for an author. I have done my best to be respectful, but if I failed, I am sorry.

THANK YOU

I have been blessed with many good friends who have provided endless chances to observe moaning in action. Some have directly contributed their theories about moaning, and others have provided days, probably months, of happy whinging, griping, complaining, moaning and occasionally ranting.

Thank you all: Angela, Barry, Brian, Caroline, Eileen, Jan, John, Keith, Kim, Paddy, Pauline, Peter, Philip, Richard, Robert, Robin, Ron, Sharon, Steve, Tony and Tommy

If anybody recognises themselves depicted in the book, then they are probably right.

Three people deserve a special 'thank you'.

My old friend Malcolm Vincent has provided me with hours, days, weeks even, of high-octane moaning. Many of his insights are incorporated into this book.

Suzanne Arnold, my editor, for her patience and magical skills in converting my words into readable English.

Finally, to Stella, my wife, for her tolerance, her thoughts about moaning, listening to my endless gripes and, above everything, for making me laugh.

GLOSSARY

ACTIVITY-BASED MOANS... Moans associated with common daily activities (e.g. driving, cycling, walking the dog).

AUDIENCE... Friends, workmates, partners – any person or group of people who the moaner converses with.

BITCHING... Moaning in a spiteful and malicious way.

BLEATING... Moaning in a pathetic and obsessive way that irritates the audience.

CARPING... Moaning about the same few subjects in an endless loop. Somebody who is overly critical and difficult to please.

DERANGEMENT SYNDROME... Triggered by certain keywords like 'Donald Trump' and 'Brexit', the sufferer becomes excitable and angry, replacing reasoned arguments with insults. No known cure exists.

DETACHED GRUMBLER... These moaners are shy and lack confidence and are in continual fear of offending their audience. They are moaning followers, never the initiator.

DISINFORMATION... False information spread intentionally.

DOOMSCROLLING... Actively searching online news sources for the most unhappy and shocking content. Sometimes known as doomsurfing.

EEYORES... Another name for Mood Hoover.

EGO BOOSTING... One of the reasons why people moan. With the aid of a supportive audience the moaner can criticise and ridicule without contradiction and providing justification. This creates a feel-good response and elevates their self-esteem.

ENERGY VAMPIRE... Another name for Mood Hoover.

EXERCISING POWER... Moaning as a means of demonstrating superiority, real or imagined.

FEELING VIRTUOUS... Moaning to admonish individuals and organisations perpetuating injustices to victims and those supporting the decaying social order. (See Victimhood moaning). The objective is to increase status and demonstrate understanding and sensitivity.

GENERIC MOANS... All types of moans that are not about personal matters.

GRIPING... Like 'carping' but more annoying to the audience.

GRUMBLING... Moaning in a way that intentionally communicates disagreement and unhappiness to the audience.

HARANGUE...A step beyond ranting, to become verbally and physically threatening. This isn't so much a moan but an act of verbal bullying.

INTENSITY (MOANING)... Moaning intensity measures the magnitude of a conversation containing critical commentary.

JUST ONE MORE THING... Their favourite moaning subjects trigger intense bouts of moaning when they jump from subject to subject in a predictable pattern. Just when they seem to have concluded they continue moaning with 'just one more thing'.

LIVE AND LET LIVE... They project themselves as being sensitive and aware, with liberal and progressive views. When riled they moan as intensely as any other group. They are motivated by exercising power and feeling virtuous.

LUBRICATING CONVERSATION... Using moaning to help initiate conversations with new acquaintances – often referred to as 'small talk'.

LUXURY MOANING... This is derived from the term 'luxury beliefs' when ideas and opinions confer status at no cost. In the context of moaning it means complaining about things that enhance a person's virtue but cost them nothing.

MALINFORMATION... Factual information shared, typically out of context, with harmful intent.

MAUNDERING... An introspective, low-energy type of moaning.

MEGA MOANER... Somebody who moans indiscriminately, not requiring feedback or confirmation. They are the stereotype used for the 'grumpy old' film and TV series.

MISINFORMATION... False information spread unintentionally.

MOANATHON... An event allowing a group of close friends to enjoy themselves and have unrestricted periods of moaning.

MOANING BUDDIES... An informal term for small groups of people who moan together in a relaxed manner.

MOANING CASCADE...When someone starts moaning about a subject that initiates a cascade of moans about other topics. The connection may be cursory, but the moaner creates their own logic of how the subjects are linked. Similar to Whataboutism.

MOOD (MOANING)...Rarely do the emotions of the moaner and their audience stay the same throughout a moaning session. Hopefully both become more relaxed. Things go wrong when the moaner becomes angrier and increasingly disgruntled. Worse still if this affects the audience. The 'mood' describes how this change unfolds.

MOOD HOOVER...It's arguable whether these people are really moaning. They view everything in a negative light, an attitude that can rapidly infect the mood of friends and colleagues. Sometimes known as Energy Vampires.

MUTTERING...Solitary moaning at a barely audible volume.

OBSESSIVE MOANER...Rather than seeking an audience to share their grievances they 'internalise' them (i.e. they talk to themselves or to inanimate objects, especially the radio and TV). Often mistaken for a Mega Moaner or a Mood Hoover, the extent and intensity of their moaning can be much greater.

ONE-TRICK PONY...These moaners habitually complain about a narrow range of subjects for reasons of ego boosting and feeling virtuous. In the unlikely case the moan is personal it results from some deeply felt hurt.

PATTERN (MOANING)...This describes the predictability of a moaning session. Each type of moaner has a unique way of subject selection – rarely is it random.

PERSONAL MOANS... Moans about personal issues. For instance, relationships, finances, work, 'big decisions' etc).

PRATTLE... An inconsequential or incomprehensible childish moaning. Sometimes known as bleating.

PROFESSIONAL MOANER... An experienced moaner with practical and theoretical knowledge of the subject. Somebody who has read *The Joy of Moaning.*

RANT... An aggressive, out-of-control variety of moaning that contains accusations devoid of any justification.

RANTER... The most extreme form of a moaner. They make no pretence to engage in orderly conversations, but instead repeat their grievances in a loud and bombastic way (ranting). Sometimes this is known as 'venting'.

RATIONAL (MOANING)... Moans can be emotional statements of criticism, with no words of substantiation. They can be the conclusion of a connected series of justified statements. This term describes the extent of rationality supporting a moan.

RED ALERTS... Used to stop moaning sessions becoming angry and argumentative. It's an agreed signal to change the subject of the conversation.

RELUCTANT MOANER... This type of moaner is overly sensitive to the opinions of others about their moaning habit. They suppress their desire to moan, only relaxing when they are with a trusted audience.

SANDBOX... Rarely do friends and workmates agree on all subjects. Rather than instinctively avoiding the contentious topics, they can be consigned to the sandbox. Everybody agrees they will be excluded from the conversation.

SIGNALLING GROUP MEMBERSHIP... Using moaning to gain acceptance by others who are in the same situation or have common interests.

SOCIAL MOANER... Moaning to gain social approval and signal group membership are the primary motivators for this type of moaner. They share many of the characteristics of the Detached Grumbler. Rather than initiating a moan, they prefer to 'go with the flow' of the conversation.

TALK-TO-LISTEN RATIO... During a conversation, the amount of time spent talking divided by the period spent listening. A concept that helps reduce the urge to talk about oneself.

TALKING THERAPY... The most intimate type of moaning that only occurs between close friends. Used to release tension and discuss personal matters. The audience adopts the role of an amateur therapist and the moaner the client.

TRANSITORY MOANS... Moaning subjects that are of seemingly immense importance one day and forgotten the next.

TYPE (MOANING)... The subjects of moans can be divided into two types. Personal moans are about those things that are specific to the individual. Generic moans cover all other subjects. Most of the time there's nothing that can be done to affect the outcome of generic moaning. Personal moans can, but rarely do, result in concrete actions.

VENTING... Another word for ranting.

VICTIMHOOD MOANING... Moans that are framed in terms of 'intersectionality', a concept that views the world as competing privileges and inequalities 'intersecting' to generate rich veins of moaning topics.

VIRTUE MOANING... When somebody moans in a conspicuous way to promote their virtue and achieve status.

WHATABOUTISM... The technique of not answering questions by asking another. For instance, 'what about the high price of property?' The response might be 'yes but what about such low interest rates?' It also refers to the way moans are linked together by the phrase 'and what about?' Similar to a moaning cascade.

WHINGING... Repetitive, monotone moaning about perceived injustices, normally of a personal type.

Printed in Great Britain
by Amazon